HORACE BUSHNELL

SOCIETY OF BIBLICAL LITERATURE
BIBLICAL SCHOLARSHIP IN NORTH AMERICA

Kent Harold Richards, Editor

JAMES O. DUKE

HORACE BUSHNELL
On the Vitality of Biblical Language

Scholars Press
Chico, California

SOCIETY OF BIBLICAL LITERATURE
CENTENNIAL PUBLICATIONS

The Society of Biblical Literature gratefully acknowledges a grant
from the National Endowment for the Humanities to underwrite
certain editorial and research expenses of the Centennial Publications Series. Published results and interpretations do not necessar-
ily represent the view of the Endowment.

© 1984
Society of Biblical Literature

Library of Congress Cataloging in Publication Data

Duke, James O.
    Horace Bushnell: on the vitality of biblical language.

    (Biblical scholarship in North America ; no. 9)
(Centennial publications / Society of Biblical Literature)
    Bibliography: p.
    1. Bible—Criticism, interpretation, etc.—History—
19th century. 2. Bushnell, Horace, 1802–1876. I. Bushnell,
Horace, 1802–1876. II. Title. III. Series. IV. Series: Cen-
tennial publications (Society of Biblical Literature)
BS500.D83   1984   22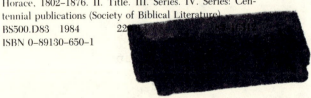
ISBN 0-89130-650-1

Printed in the United States of America

CONTENTS

ACKNOWLEDGMENTS

In the writing of this modest-sized monograph I have run up a number of academic debts which, I am thankful, are of the sort that I am delighted to acknowledge. For the opportunity to contribute to the Centennial Publications of the Society of Biblical Literature, I wish to express my gratitude to the editorial board. A special word of thanks is due Kent Richards, Maurya Horgan, Brooks Holifield, and Douglas Knight, each of whom has donated valuable time so that this project might move from proposal to press.

This work has benefited from the comments of some perspicacious readers. Two of my colleagues at Brite Divinity School, William Countryman and Toni Craven, offered helpful suggestions at a very early and critical stage of drafting. The counsel offered by Conrad Cherry, Director of Scholars Press and a wise historian of American religious history, has been invaluable.

My study of Bushnell materials at the library of Yale Divinity School was made at once productive and pleasant by the cooperation of Leander Keck, Dean of the Divinity School, Stephen Peterson, the Divinity School Librarian, and Martha Lund Smalley, a most able archivist. I wish also to thank Janna Ferguson of the Interlibrary Loan Department of the Mary Couts Burnett Library of Texas Christian University for her exceptional efforts in behalf of my research. To my two typists, Iris Valdez and Ann Chambers, and to my research assistants, Doug Goodwin, Cassandra Duke, and Carol Schneider, I am most grateful.

My obligation to Robert W. Funk is in a class by itself. It was he who, some fourteen years ago, introduced me to *Hermeneutik*, who helped guide my passage from graduate school to full-time teaching and research, who prompted me to extend my interests from the European to the American theater, and who conferred with me about my initial proposal for this volume. Throughout it all, his own work at the frontiers of biblical, theological, and religious studies has been for me unfailingly thought-provoking and instructive.

I have had the good fortune to receive encouragement and support from M. Jack Suggs, the Dean of Brite Divinity School. Financial aid for this project has come from the National Endowment for the Humanities and from the Research Committee of Texas Christian University.

I

INTRODUCTION

If and when a much-needed general history of biblical scholarship in America is forthcoming, it will have to reckon with Horace Bushnell (1802–1876), whose career as a Congregationalist minister spanned the middle years of the nineteenth century and signalized a turning point in American Protestant thought. Pastor of North Church in Hartford, Connecticut, from 1833 until 1859, when ill health forced him to relinquish his position in favor of a self-styled "ministry at large," Bushnell was and is best known as an early princeling of the pulpit, a pioneer in Christian education, a theologian, and a commentator on the spiritual state of the nation. His performance in these roles has gained for him numerous, and mixed, reviews.[1] Relatively little, however, has been said about his activities as a

---

[1] Mary Bushnell Cheyney, *The Life and Letters of Horace Bushnell* (New York: Harper and Brothers, 1880) 471. The bibliography of literature on Bushnell is vast and still growing; only a few recent studies can be mentioned here. Overviews of his life and work are given by William R. Adamson (*Bushnell Rediscovered* [Boston: United Church Press, 1966]) and by Barbara M. Cross (*Horace Bushnell: Minister to a Changing America* [Chicago: University of Chicago Press, 1958]). General estimates of his career in the context of American religious history can be found in Sydney Ahlstrom, *A Religious History of the American People* (New Haven: Yale University Press, 1972) 609–13; idem, ed., *Theology in America* (Indianapolis and New York: Bobbs-Merrill, 1967) 62–64, 317–19; Nelson R. Burr. *A Critical Bibliography of Religion in America* (Princeton Studies in American Civilization, 5; Princeton: Princeton University Press, 1961); William A. Clebsch, *American Religious Thought: A History* (Chicago History of American Religion; Chicago: University of Chicago Press, 1973) 114–23; Ernest Trice Thompson, "Horace Bushnell and the Beginning of American Liberalism," *Changing Emphases in American Preaching* (Philadelphia: Westminster, 1943) 4–49.

On Bushnell's theology see also Conrad Cherry, *Nature and the Religious Imagination: From Edwards to Bushnell* (Philadelphia: Fortress, 1980) chaps. 8–10; David L. Smith, *Symbolism and Growth: The Religious Thought of Horace Bushnell* (AAR Dissertation Series, 36; Chico, CA: Scholars Press, 1981); H. Shelton Smith, ed., *Horace Bushnell: Twelve Selections* (Library of Protestant Thought; New York: Oxford University Press, 1965); Claude Welch, *Protestant Thought in the Nineteenth Century.* Vol. 1: *1799–1870* (New Haven: Yale University Press, 1972) 258–68.

Although the Massachusetts Sabbath School Society withdrew its publication of Bushnell's sermons on Christian nurture (*Discourses on Christian Nurture* [Boston, 1847]), interest in Bushnell's view of Christian education (the complete work was entitled *Christian Nurture* [New York: Charles Scribner, 1861]) has remained strong; see, e.g., Garland Knott, "Bushnell Revisited," *Religious Education* 64 (1969) 291–95; John H. Krahn,

student of the Bible, how they figure in the history of biblical studies, and how they illumine that history.[2] This essay attempts to shed a ray of light on these questions.

Bushnell was not a specialist in the field of Bible. He neither expected nor received an academic post in biblical studies, and his research, which was invariably geared to urgent homiletical and theological needs, did not gain him any acclaim as an expert in the biblical disciplines. Yet if those interested in the history of biblical scholarship take account of the setting within which it developed, the assumptions on which it was based, and the goals toward which it pressed, they will not overlook Bushnell's work.

Throughout the nineteenth century the context of religious inquiry was transformed by strong sociocultural forces—aftershocks of the Enlightenment, advances in scientific knowledge, shifting philosophical

---

"Nurture versus Revival: Horace Bushnell on Religious Education," *Religious Education* 70 (1975) 375–82; Randolph Crump Miller, "Horace Bushnell: Prophet to America's Children," *Perkins Journal* 32 (1979) 1–8; David S. Steward, "Bushnell's Nurture Process: An Exposition," *Religious Education* 64 (1969) 296–302; idem, "Horace Bushnell and Contemporary Christian Education: A Study of Revelation and Nurture" (Ph.D. diss., Yale University, 1966).

On Bushnell's social thought, see H. A. Barnes, "The Idea that Caused a War: Horace Bushnell versus Thomas Jefferson," *Journal of Church and State* 16 (1974) 73–83; Conrad Cherry, "The Structure of Organic Thinking: Horace Bushnell's Approach to Language, Nature, and Nation," *JAAR* 40 (1972) 3–20; William A. Clebsch, *Christian Interpretations of the Civil War* (Philadelphia: Fortress, 1969); Charles C. Cole, Jr., "Horace Bushnell and the Slavery Question," *New England Quarterly* 23 (1950) 19–30; idem, *The Social Ideas of the Northern Evangelists, 1826–1860* (New York: Columbia University Press, 1954); Charles H. Hopkins, *The Rise of the Social Gospel in American Protestantism, 1865–1915* (Yale Studies in Religious Education, 14; New Haven: Yale University Press, 1940); Randolph Crump Miller, "A State Renewed in Righteousness," *Perkins Journal* 32 (1979) 17–25; Lewis Weeks, "Horace Bushnell on Black America," *Religious Education* 68 (1973) 28–41. Also of significance are the scattered references to Bushnell given by Ann Douglas, *The Feminization of American Culture* (New York; Alfred A. Knopf, 1977); George M. Fredrickson, *The Black Image in the White Mind* (New York: Harper and Row, 1971); idem, *The Inner Civil War* (New York: Harper and Row, 1965).

[2] In the course of dealing with Bushnell's theory of religious symbolism, most commentators make at least passing reference to his approach to biblical literature, but there has been no sustained treatment of the topic. The indispensable survey of antebellum biblical scholarship in the North is Jerry Wayne Brown, *The Rise of Biblical Criticism in America, 1800–1870: The New England Scholars* (Middletown, CT: Wesleyan University Press, 1969), which devotes only a few pages to Bushnell. Brief but helpful discussions of Bushnell's view of biblical-theological language are included in Cherry, *Nature and the Religious Imagination*; Donald A. Crosby, *Horace Bushnell's Theory of Language, in the Context of Other Nineteenth-Century Philosophies of Language* (The Hague: Mouton, 1975); Charles Feidelson, *Symbolism and American Literature* (Chicago: University of Chicago Press, 1953) 151–57; Eddie Bong Lo, "Horace Bushnell's Religious Epistemology in Relation to his Major Christian Doctrines: A Historical, Philosophical, and Theological Consideration" (Ph.D. diss., Claremont College, 1977) 171–91; Randolph Crump Miller, "God's Gift to the Imagination," *Perkins Journal* 32 (1979) 9–16; D. L. Smith, *Symbolism and Growth*, 107–29.

currents, changing patterns of social relations, and the processes of nation building, to name only a few. Christians faced crucial decisions with regard to their allegiances, and for many evangelical Protestants, including Bushnell, the confrontation prompted a restless search for some way to reconcile the heritage of Calvinism with the exigencies of modern life. The passage of New England theology from the Edwardsean era to the various liberalisms that flourished at the end of the nineteenth century illustrates where that search could lead. Among the manifold adjustments made in this passage came reappraisals of the proper treatment of the Bible, that is, new proposals regarding its authority, its interpretation, and its uses for theology. The course of biblical scholarship in America cannot rightly be understood apart from this context. And since Bushnell was by all accounts one of the foremost adjusters of the era, it is both fitting and instructive to consider his proposals for the treatment of the Bible and the brand of biblical study attached to them.

That Bushnell was a transitional figure in nineteenth-century Protestantism there is no doubt. His reputation, such as it is, has always been based on his reformulations of what passed for orthodoxy and his anticipations of what was to become liberalism. Yet exactly how to plot his position along this trajectory is something of a historiographical puzzle.[3] He does not fit snugly into any of the established New England schools and he founded none of his own. He had first-hand acquaintance with stricter and milder forms of Calvinism, the first from his early church experience and the second from his seminary training under Nathaniel W. Taylor and the cadre of "New Haven theologians" at Yale Divinity School. He nonetheless withheld his full endorsement from either party. Like the Unitarians, with whom he was in considerable sympathy, he complained that the theologies of orthodoxy did harm to Christianity by presenting it in terms that conflicted with the sensibilities of thoughtful, cultured Americans. His contemporaries, it would seem, viewed him as a

---

[3] In *A Genetic History of the New England Theology* (New York: Russell & Russell, 1907), Frank Hugh Foster placed Bushnell among the "Later New Haven Theologians," and in *The Modern Movement in American Theology* (New York: Fleming H. Revell, 1939), he listed Theodore Munger and James Whiton as members of Bushnell's school. Claude Welch (*Protestant Thought*, 144, 192), however, notes that Bushnell is among those nineteenth-century figures who defy precise labeling. Williston Walker, who noted the extent of Bushnell's influence on late nineteenth-century thought, nonetheless wrote, "he founded no school in the technical sense. No party among us calls itself by his name" ("Dr. Bushnell as a Religious Leader," *Bushnell Centenary: Minutes of the General Association of Connecticut* [Hartford: Case, Lockwood and Brainard, 1902] 34). See also Cyrus A. Bartol, "Dr. Horace Bushnell and the Quandaries of our Theology," *Unitarian Review* 14 (1880) 244; and George Park Fisher, "Horace Bushnell," *International Review* 10 (1881) 13. The independence of thought evident in Bushnell and those influenced by him hardly allows for anything more than a rough classification. See also A. David Bos, "Horace Bushnell through his Interpreters," *Andover Newton Quarterly* 18 (1977) 122–32.

maverick who roamed in the theological wonderland to the left of New
Haven Calvinism and to the right of Boston Unitarianism. Conservatives
within his denomination tried to expel him from the ministry, but he
managed to remain a Congregationalist to the end and refused to go by
any name other than "orthodox."[4] His plea for a comprehensive Christianity that admitted a germ of truth in every theology but transcended
them all won him few sympathizers, and in his lonely moments he took
consolation in the thought "My day has not yet come, and will not till
after I am gone."[5]

The passing of time has not made it any easier to classify him. So many
Bushnellian attitudes and themes became commonplace in the liberalisms
that developed after his death that some have been inclined to laud him as
a seer, a liberator, or a prophet of the future.[6] Yet even those who praise his
progressivism must admit that his vision was limited.[7] His emphasis on the
organic solidarity of family, church, and nation did not ripen into a genu-
inely social gospel. His respect for scientific progress did not extend to Dar-
win's theory of evolution. His determination to free theology from the grip
of dogmatism did not lead him to embrace historical criticism. A Janus, he
had one face turned to the future and one to the past.

From today's perspective, nineteenth-century conservatisms and liberalisms alike bear the unmistakable impress of cultural conditioning. Thus
Bushnell's pose would seem to betoken the ambivalences of a religious tradition and a social order in a time of travail.[8] There is justice in this verdict.
But Bushnell is not to be dismissed as a mere victim of circumstances. His

---

[4] Cheyney, *Life and Letters*, 338: "We must remember that Dr. Bushnell had never
ceased to consider himself orthodox according to the ancient standards; in fact, that he
felt it to be his mission to rescue certain important truths of orthodoxy from the mire into
which they had fallen." See ibid., 258–59, 339, 414, for Bushnell's own remarks on the
topic. It would be best to say that he had no interest in orthodoxy as a party but wished to
preserve the "substance" of historic Christianity. A study of Bushnell's doctrine of the
Trinity made by Frederick Kirschenmann ("Horace Bushnell: Orthodox or Sabellian?"
Church History 33 [1964] 49–59) provides a good test case.

[5] Cheyney, *Life and Letters*, 420.

[6] Bushnell the "seer" is mentioned by Foster (*Modern Movement in American Theology*, 59), the "liberator," by John W. Buckham (*Progressive Religious Thought in America* [Boston: Houghton, Mifflin, 1919] 32); the "prophet," by Edwin Pond Parker ("Horace
Bushnell: Christian Prophet," in *Bushnell Centenary*, 86–99). In *Realistic Theology* (New
York: Harper and Brothers, 1934), Walter Marshall Horton calls Bushnell "the Schleiermacher of America" (p. 27) and claims with satisfaction, "the theology of Bushnell is
essentially identical with the liberal theology which is passing away before our eyes"
(p. 30).

[7] See, e.g., Foster, *Modern Movement in American Theology*, 59–61; A. J. William
Myers, *Horace Bushnell and Religious Education* (Boston: Manthorne and Burdock,
1937) 104.

[8] This is the thrust of Clebsch, *American Religious Thought*, 114–23; Cross, *Horace
Bushnell*, 158–59; and Douglas, *Feminization of American Culture*.

response to countervailing pressures was passive–aggressive and always highly individual. He dreamed of being a great reconciler, but not a great compromiser in the manner of Henry Clay.[9] In his opinion everything— Trinitarianism and Unitarianism, Calvinism and Arminianism, Christianity and culture, the natural and the supernatural—combined to form a whole that was greater than the sum of its parts.

Emerson could announce, "there are always two parties, the party of the past and the party of the future, the Establishment and the Movement,"[10] and for a while at least he could give himself unstintingly to the Movement. Bushnell denied that life came down to an either/or:

> In the question of old and new, perpetually recurring in matters of religion, we have the bigot on one side asserting that nothing may be new, and the radical on the other, that nothing shall be old. And if Christianity be a vital power in the church, both are true; for the new must be the birth of the old, and the old must have its births, or die.[11]

This inability to choose either "to make a future identical with the past, or to make a future separate from the past" may reflect some flaw in Bushnell's personality.[12] But he himself would have one believe that there was a principle at stake: "as finite beings we are always at a point between the past and the future, having one behind us and the other before us, and a most real and valid connection with both, with one by memory, with the other by some anticipative exercise in the nature of prophecy."[13]

This assessment of the historicality of human existence led Bushnell to assert that "the future must be of the past, and the past must create a future."[14] Only when "bigots" and "radicals" could "coalesce in some

[9] His vision was best stated in "Christian Comprehensiveness," first published in 1848 and reprinted in *Building Eras in Religion* (Literary Varieties, III; New York: Charles Scribner's Sons, 1881) 387–459. It was the service of H. Shelton Smith (*Horace Bushnell*, 106–8) to highlight the significance of this theme. See also Irving H. Bartlett, "Bushnell, Cousin, and Comprehensive Christianity," *Journal of Religion* (1957) 99–104; and Harold R. Heiniger, "The Theological Technique of a Mediating Theologian—Horace Bushnell" (Ph.D. diss., University of Chicago, 1935). In *Protestant Thought* (p. 28), Welch notes that Bushnell sought a critical orthodoxy that would not be a mere compromise or an amalgamation of divergent viewpoints. The unapproved use of one of Bushnell's sermons during the election campaign of 1844 led him to publish the work in order to make clear his opinion of Clay, the great compromiser; see *Politics under the Law of God* (Hartford: E. Hunt, 1844).

[10] Ralph Waldo Emerson, *The Complete Works* (ed. Edward A. Emerson; New York: William H. Wise, 1923) 10:325.

[11] Bushnell, "Christian Comprehensiveness," *Building Eras in Religion*, 421.

[12] Ibid.

[13] Horace Bushnell, "Unconscious Prophecy," *The Spirit in Man: Sermons and Selections* (New York: Charles Scribner's Sons, 1903) 54.

[14] Bushnell, "Christian Comprehensiveness," *Building Eras in Religion*, 421.

common result" would the "right view" be found, and this required a firm grasp of the "real and valid connection" between past and future.[15] Confident that religious feeling, sound personal character, and the quickening of the divine spirit could join what theological opinion making had cast asunder, Bushnell sometimes skirted tough intellectual decisions. At other times, however, he resolutely set out to rebuild theological foundations for a house large enough to hold both the party of memory and the party of hope.[16]

These preliminary remarks, as schematic as they are, set the stage for dealing with Bushnell's proposals for the treatment of the Bible. The proposals were part of an overall program of theological reform which partook of elements old and new. Bushnell's interest in the Bible, and in biblical scholarship, stemmed from a desire to formulate a tenable theology, and both the desire and the attempt to satisfy it were shaped by disputes among evangelicals, Unitarians, transcendentalists, and skeptics about what constituted "tenability" and "theology." Much the same, of course, must be said of most every other contributor to biblical studies in the nineteenth century, so long as one acknowledges that the points in dispute no less than the disputants were constantly changing. In the absence of an independent academic tradition, the study of the Bible was inextricably bound up with rivalries about religion, and the biblical investigations of nineteenth-century scholars were anything but "disinterested." That Bushnell aligned his own biblical studies with a program of theology would be a fact hardly worth noting if the alignment had not been so peculiar.

Its peculiarity is perhaps most evident at the point of hermeneutics, especially since it has become customary to associate liberal theologies with historical-critical biblical scholarship. To be sure, the association can no longer be taken for granted as it once was, for interpretation theory is again in ferment in this "post-critical age." It is therefore an opportune time to note that in Bushnell's day the situation was far more fluid than it was during the battles between fundamentalists and liberals. In an effort to improve upon religious arguments based on uncritical, dogmatic readings of the Bible, a number of American religious intellectuals between 1800 and 1860 had begun to import the critical biblical studies available in Europe, and especially in Germany, and to manufacture them at home.[17]

---

15 Ibid.

16 Drawing upon Emerson's terminology, R. W. B. Lewis (*The American Adam: Innocence, Tragedy, and Tradition in the Nineteenth Century* [Chicago: University of Chicago Press, 1955] 7–8) refers to the two parties and places Bushnell within a third group, which manifested an ironic temperament of tragic optimism.

17 Brown, *Biblical Criticism in America*. On the leading evangelical scholar who is sometimes called the founder of American biblical criticism, see John Giltner, "Moses Stuart, 1770–1852" (Ph.D. diss., Yale University, 1965).

In principle, if not in practice, these studies suspended dogmatic preconceptions about the Bible and subjected it to the same kinds of philological, literary, and historical examination applied to other ancient documents. The analyses of texts, language studies, commentaries, and discussions of biblical geography and history that appeared on the American scene in this period marked the beginnings of the indigenization of scholarly traditions, which would by the end of the century gain ascendancy in many American churches and colleges.

Whatever their intrinsic value, these critical studies fed directly into a number of hermeneutical options that served theological purposes: the determination of purely grammatical meaning, apart from judgments about the truth of that meaning, as set down by Ernesti; grammatico-historical criticism, which—as developed by disciples of Ernesti and Semler—considered both the language and the subject matter of the biblical texts in light of their historical setting and rational intelligibility; and more or less fully historical-critical methods, as suggested by Semler and extended by the like of Michaelis, Eichhorn, Schleiermacher, De Wette, and Strauss.[18] Mindful that critical studies could challenge time-honored religious opinions, most American practitioners in this early period took care to draw the line at "irresponsible" applications and "destructive" conclusions.

This was a line, however, that could be drawn, and redrawn, depending on circumstances. The trustees of Andover Seminary, for example, feared the introduction of any German criticism. But in the hands of Moses Stuart, Andover's premier biblical scholar, the principles of grammatico-historical study proved with rare exception only to confirm traditional judgments. The Unitarian George R. Noyes ventured beyond grammatico-historical criticism to entertain historical-critical doubts about the Old Testament; yet he stopped short of skepticism about the gospels. Only

---

[18] See in addition to the works noted above: Theodore Dwight Bozeman, *Protestantism in an Age of Science: The Baconian Ideal and Antebellum American Religious Thought* (Chapel Hill: University of North Carolina Press, 1977) chap. 7; Jürgen Herbst, *The German Historical School in American Scholarship* (Ithaca, NY: Cornell University Press, 1965) chap. 4; Brooks Holifield, *The Gentlemen Theologians: American Theology in Southern Culture, 1795–1860* (Durham, NC: Duke University Press, 1978) 96–100; Herbert Hovenkamp, *Science and Religion in America, 1800–1860* (Philadelphia: University of Pennsylvania Press, 1978) 57–78; Loefferts Loetscher, *The Broadening Church* (Philadelphia: University of Pennsylvania Press, 1954) chap. 3; Harold Y. Vanderpool, "The Andover Conservatives: Apologetics, Biblical Criticism, and Theological Change at Andover Theological Seminary, 1808–1880" (Ph.D. diss., Harvard University, 1971).

On the European backgrounds of these hermeneutical options see, especially Wilhelm Dilthey, *Gesammelte Schriften*. Vol. 14,2: *Leben Schleiermachers* (ed. Martin Redeker; Göttingen: Vandenhoeck & Ruprecht, 1966) 627–84; and Hans Frei, *The Eclipse of Biblical Narrative: A Study in Eighteenth and Nineteenth Century Hermeneutics* (New Haven: Yale University Press, 1974) chaps. 6, 8–10.

Theodore Parker, "the most radical critic in America," had a kind word to say for the *Leben Jesu* of Strauss—an opinion consonant with Parker's own plan to clear away the positivity of Christianity so that absolute religion might burgeon.[19] Since Bushnell repudiated dogmatic interpretation and wished to show the compatibility between Christianity and modern scientific inquiry, there is reason to wonder why, as Jerry Wayne Brown has put it, his connection with critical studies was only "slight."[20]

The slightness of the connection is not to be blamed on a failure of nerve, a devotional blind spot, or a precritical naiveté. Bushnell was not without such weaknesses, but to explain his approach to the Bible on this basis is to oversimplify the situation. He did, after all, launch frontal assaults against many cherished, and entrenched, theological positions, and his own way of interpreting the Bible was no less controversial than that of many who took keen interest in critical studies. Nor was he blissfully ignorant of scholarly trends, as Brown would have one believe when he says that "[Bushnell's] writings reveal no awareness of biblical studies in Germany or of the critical opinions of American scholars."[21] Brown himself admits that Bushnell knew of the linguistic studies of Josiah Willard Gibbs and "distinguished himself by applying them to the Bible and to religious language."[22] But Bushnell also responded directly to the estimates of the gospels given by Parker, Strauss, and Hennell.[23] Furthermore, even if one could separate the critical opinions about the Bible from the theological conclusions reached by those with whom Bushnell sparred, Bushnell certainly made no such distinction. His quarrel with modern biblical interpreters extended to the critics as well as the dogmatists. Indeed, since critical studies were used on the one hand by the orthodox and the Unitarians to support their (opposing) theological claims and on the other hand by "radicals" like Parker to move above, if not beyond, historic Christianity, the difference between a "critic" and a "dogmatist" was by no means clear-cut.

Bushnell was not an anticritical traditionalist, and he was certainly open to new ideas. Jerry Wayne Brown comes close to the heart of the matter when he observes that Bushnell's expropriation of the linguistic ideas of Gibbs "tended to make Gibbs's biblical studies seem unnecessary." But in claiming that "a strong dependence upon intuition, inspiration, and sympathy to interpret a biblical text made study of original languages, investigations of authorship, and historical reconstruction unimportant,"

---

[19] Brown. *Biblical Criticism in America*, chaps. 3, 6, 8–10.

[20] Ibid., 171.

[21] Ibid.

[22] Ibid., 177.

[23] See below, chap. 7. See William Johnson, *Nature and the Supernatural in the Theology of Horace Bushnell* (Studia Theologica Lundensia, 25; Lund: CWK Gleerup, 1963) chap. 3.

Brown misleadingly singles out only one facet of Bushnell's proposal for biblical interpretation.[24] It would be more accurate to say that Bushnell's overall conception of linguistic communication would not permit dogmatic, grammatical, or historical criticisms to determine the meaning of texts. Thus his proposal is a curiosity in that it forsook precritical dogmatism without resorting to what later liberals took to be the only alternative—the methodology of historical criticism.

If later liberals did not know what to make of Bushnell's disinterest in critical scholarship, religious partisans of his own day were at least equally perplexed by his views on the authority and uses of the Bible in theology. In order to demonstrate that the past could create a future, Bushnell undertook "a reordering of the theological enterprise comparable to the work of Schleiermacher or Hegel or Coleridge."[25] This effort involved among other things a rethinking of the meaning of revelation and what Claude Welch has called the "decisive Socratic turn to the self," which meant that "theology now had to start from, to articulate, and to interpret a subjective view of the religious object."[26] The fact that these moves were to become taken-for-granted assumptions among post-Kantian liberals should not lead anyone to discount their significance. Although it is highly unlikely that Bushnell ever read a word of Kant, he was nonetheless one of the very first Americans to respond to the "Copernican revolution" in theology. His reading of Coleridge's *Aids to Reflection* was evidently the major stimulus for his thinking, and in light of his references to other European sources (in English translation!) such as Cousin, Schleiermacher, Rothe, Tholuck, and Neander, he was clearly attuned to, if hardly dependent upon or well versed in, literature from the age of idealism and romanticism.[27] His mastery of modern theological

---

24 Brown, *Biblical Criticism in America*, 179.

25 Welch, *Protestant Thought*, 127.

26 Ibid., 59–60.

27 A cautious comment on the degree to which Bushnell knew of and learned from post-Kantian developments in European theology is made by David Smith, *Symbolism and Growth*, 6–25. Acknowledging that "from one point of view, Bushnell's romanticism is vibrant and pervasive," Smith rightly notes (p. 23) that it is hard to ascertain precisely how extensively Bushnell had read and appropriated the literature of the period. He also calls attention to both the Puritan and the eighteenth-century background of Bushnell's view of symbol, analogy, and typology.

On Bushnell's connection with romantic and idealist themes, see Ahlstrom, *Religious History of the American People*, 609–13; Robert D. Baird, "Religion is Life: An Inquiry into the Dominating Motif in the Theology of Horace Bushnell" (Ph.D. diss., State University of Iowa, 1964); Irving H. Bartlett, "The Romantic Theology of Horace Bushnell" (Ph.D. diss., Brown University, 1952); Mildred Kitto Billings, "The Theology of Horace Bushnell Considered in Relation to That of Samuel Taylor Coleridge" (Ph.D. diss., University of Chicago, 1960); L. C. Foard, "The Copernican Revolution in Theology: Studies of the Critical and Romantic Elements in the Theory of Religious Language Proposed by Horace Bushnell" (Ph.D. diss., Temple University, 1970).

scholarship did not compare with that of the Mercersburg theologians or that of Parker, but his ability to weave threads old and new into American whole cloth was second to none, and in this respect at least he was to be a role model for many later evangelical liberals.[28]

In Bushnell's scheme of things, primacy was given to the inner experience of the presence of God in the life of the believer. This experience, a God-consciousness, founded and fostered the growth of character, that is, a process that moved toward an inward self-integrity and self-fulfillment according to God's design for humanity. The various elements of the Christian religion, including the Bible, were to be understood, evaluated, and handled in terms of their contribution to this process. Thus Bushnell proposed to vest the authority of the Bible in its capacity to play a constitutive role in the formation of Christian character. Biblical interpretation was to be what may be called an "aesthetic engagement" between the text and the interpreter, culminating in an "existential" knowledge of God. The theologian was to make use of the Bible primarily by drawing upon its fund of linguistic resources in order to express and expand religious consciousness.

The chief aim of this essay is to explicate Bushnell's proposals for the treatment of the Bible. Attention is given first to the concept of revelation, which was determinative for his entire program and which permitted him to approach the Bible as "the grand poem of salvation"[29] (chapter 2). Consideration then turns to his theory of language (chapter 3) and to his account of the task of biblical interpretation (chapter 4). There follows a resume of his understanding of the authority and use of the Bible for theology (chapter 5), which is illustrated by reference to three topics—the disclosive power of the word "sin" (chapter 6), the character of Jesus as "God's last metaphor"[30] (chapter 7), and the work of Christ (chapter 8). The path from exegesis to homiletics is then traced by looking at his handling of some Pauline materials dealing with justification and life "in Christ" (chapter 9). These discussions are not meant to add up to an exhaustive analysis of Bushnell's theology as a whole or even of

---

[28] In addition to the works cited in nn. 3, 6–7 above, see William R. Hutchison, *The Modernist Impulse in American Protestantism* (Cambridge: Harvard University Press, 1976) 41–48; Hopkins, *Rise of the Social Gospel*, 5, 318; Williston Walker, "Changes in Theology among American Congregationalists," *American Journal of Theology* 10 (1906) 204–18.

Special tribute was paid to Bushnell's influence by Washington Gladden, "Horace Bushnell and Progressive Orthodoxy," *Pioneers of Religious Liberty in America* (Boston: American Unitarian Association, 1903) 227–63; idem, *Recollections* (Boston: Houghton, Mifflin; Cambridge: Riverside, 1909) 118–20, 165–68; Theodore Munger, *Horace Bushnell, Preacher and Theologian* (Boston: Houghton, Mifflin, 1899) 118–20, 165–68; H. Clay Trumbull, *My Four Religious Teachers* (Philadelphia: Sunday School Times, 1903) 70–125.

[29] Bushnell, *God in Christ* (Hartford: Brown and Parsons, 1849) 74.

[30] Bushnell, "Our Gospel A Gift to the Imagination," *Building Eras in Religion*, 259.

his range of thinking on these particular discussions. Within this space, it must be sufficient to identify and to probe the treatment accorded a variety of biblical texts and themes.

Each of Bushnell's proposals was predicated on a dialectical relationship between language and experience: Language gives form to experience; experience gives meaning to linguistic form. The dialectic was conceived as a lively interplay between the language of the past and the experience of the present, such that biblical language might impinge upon the life of its readers and that its readers—if they "set in upon the text with a tidal pressure of living affinities"—would be drawn by the language to new "discoveries" and "depths."[31] In general, therefore, Bushnell's treatment of the Bible represented his determination to promote "the vitality of biblical language." Convinced that neither dogmatic nor critical studies could do justice to the "significatory power" of scripture, he pursued a brand of biblical study oriented to a literary–aesthetic–religious appreciation of biblical language. Many of Bushnell's aims, attitudes, tactics, and proposals were accepted by the generations of liberals who came after him. His judgment on biblical study was not. Why this was so cannot be taken up in this brief essay on Bushnell himself. But one suspects that even had his hermeneutics of imaginative engagement not been riddled with so many internal difficulties, it would nonetheless have fallen as a victim of the crossfire of conservatives and liberals who disputed the relationship between the language and the subject matter of the Bible. The story of Bushnell's proposals for the treatment of the Bible and the type of biblical study associated with them forms a curious episode in the history of American biblical scholarship, worthy of attention because it affords a glimpse of a nineteenth-century attempt to overcome dogmatism without falling prey to historicism.

[31] Cheyney, *Life and Letters*, 430–31.

II

THE RHETORIC OF REVELATION

It was predictable, if not inevitable, that Bushnell's program for theological reform and hence his proposals for the treatment of the Bible would hinge on the category of revelation. Conflict among traditionalist, pietistic, and enlightenment thinkers stretching back to the dawn of the eighteenth century had already advanced the topic to the head of the theological agenda. Opinions on the matter ranged of course from truculent dogmatism on the one hand to utter skepticism on the other. But in America, as in England, debate ordinarily moved within the boundaries first set by John Locke's inquiries into human understanding and later adjusted, but not removed, by Scottish Common Sense philosophy. The rules governing the discussion were primarily epistemological. Sooner or later anyone who gave serious thought to religion was pressed to weigh the relative merits of reason and revelation as sources of knowledge and to opine whether the "truths" of Christianity were in accord with, contrary to, or above reason. The legitimacy of traditional references to "revealed religion" and "biblical revelation" was put to the question.[1]

---

[1] John Locke's *Essay Concerning Human Understanding* (1690) (ed. A. S. Pringle-Pattison; Oxford: Clarendon, 1924) and his 1695 discussion of religion in *The Reasonableness of Christianity* (ed. I. T. Ramsey; Stanford: Stanford University Press, 1958) helped usher in the Enlightenment in England, and the British empirical tradition decisively shaped by his work dominated philosophy and theology throughout the eighteenth century there and in America. The appeal to common sense, basic to Scottish realism, modified the empirical tradition in order to fend off sensationalism, skepticism, and radical accounts of natural religion. John Witherspoon, who in 1768 became president of the College of New Jersey (later Princeton), was probably the first influential figure to promote the Scottish enlightenment in the American colonies.

On the intellectual context of American religious thought in the late eighteenth and the early nineteenth century, some of the most helpful recent sources are Ahlstrom, *Religious History of the American People*, chaps. 22–26; idem, "The Scottish Philosophy and American Theology," *Church History* 24 (1955) 257–71; Bozeman, *Protestantism in an Age of Science*, chap. 1; Merle Curti, "The Great Mr. Locke: America's Philosopher, 1783–1871," *Huntingdon Library Bulletin* 11 (1937) 107–55; Hovenkamp, *Science and Religion in America*, chap. 1; Henry F. May, *The Enlightenment in America* (New York: Oxford University Press, 1976) 346–58; Herbert W. Schneider, *A History of American Philosophy* (2d ed.; New York: Columbia University Press, 1963) chaps. 2–4. The emergence of the question of faith and history came with the influence of Kantian, idealist, and romantic currents of thought and brought with it a thorough reexamination of the

During the eighteenth century strong protests against these references came from rationalists, such as deists, who insisted that human
reason alone could ascertain the essential truths of religion and morality.
The existence of the Creator-God, the benevolent design of the universe,
the principles of obligation toward God and neighbor, moral accountability in this world and the next—these were cardinal tenets of the
natural religion that commended itself to universal assent. A special,
supernatural revelation such as that commonly claimed for the Bible was
adjudged neither necessary nor valid. Insofar as biblically revealed truths
were in accord with reason, they added nothing of significance to
natural religion; insofar as they were contrary to or above reason, they
could lay no claim to credibility.[2]

The prevalence of such hard-core rationalism in America should not
be overemphasized.[3] Nonetheless, the critique and the alternative offered by deists grew out of the kind of religious questioning that the
more educated classes, including the clergy, could not avoid. That questioning did not lead inevitably to conclusions hostile to "historic Christianity." Many Christians were eager to defend revealed religion by an
apologetics fit for an age beholden to Newton and Locke. Although infi-
nitely varied in detail, the apologetical model itself was simple: rational
argument could persuasively, if not absolutely, demonstrate that a special revelation was a necessary supplement to the religion of reason and
that Christianity supplied this revelation. This position, sometimes called
"rational supernaturalism" or "supernatural rationalism," concentrated its
forces at the point of theological prolegomenon. Natural theology, reha-
bilitated to meet contemporary scientific standards, was once again
pressed into service, and ever-increasing reliance was placed upon the
"evidences" of Christianity, both external and internal. Evidentiary
appeals were exceedingly diverse. In general, however, it can be said
that evidences external to the Bible were those "facts" of nature and
history (e.g., antiquity, authorship, and historical reliability of the biblical texts, miracles, and proof-from-prophecy) which attested to the genuineness of special revelation. Internal evidences were those characteristics
of biblical teachings (e.g., their clarity, consistency, and profundity),
which conformed them to the needs, conditions, and aspirations of the
human spirit. With these weapons a host of Christian intellectuals set out

---

nature of revelation; see Welch, *Protestant Thought*, 22–55, 141–46.

[2] On American deism see, in addition to the works cited above, Gustav A. Koch, *Repub-
lican Religion: The American Revolution and the Cult of Reason* (New York: Henry
Holt, 1933) and Herbert M. Morais, *Deism in Eighteenth-Century America* (New York:
Columbia University Press, 1934).

[3] Conrad Wright, *The Liberal Christians: Essays in American Unitarian History* (Boston: Beacon, 1970) 1–6.

to win the minds of thoughtful Americans.[4]

Although deistic rationalism did not thrive in post-revolutionary America, the apologetics of rational supernaturalism remained popular throughout the antebellum era and survived in some places, such as Princeton Theological Seminary, long thereafter. It was put to use in the churches, colleges, and writings of Christians with little in common except a willingness to combat doubt and indifference by intellectually reputable means. The popularity of the model was surely due in large measure to its adaptability. Strict Presbyterian confessionalists at Princeton might marshal evidences to show that the Bible in its entirety should be regarded as the divinely inspired, and therefore inerrant, depository of revealed truth. Boston Unitarians might be content with evidences substantiating the authenticity of the gospels.[5] Between the extremes lay countless middle-of-the-road options. In any case, once apologetics had demonstrated the credibility of revealed religion, the theologians were free to arrive at a determination of the content of that revelation as they thought best. Differing evaluations of scripture, creed, philosophy, science, and testimonies of religious experience led to differing determinations of that content, and squabbles among and within the churches proceeded more or less as usual. But only more or less. Preoccupation with revelation as a source of information about history, precepts, and morals gave a new accent and a new twist to the abiding concern for sound doctrine. It tended to accentuate the importance of theological

[4] Ibid., 6–21. See also Ahlstrom, "Scottish Philosophy"; Bozeman, *Protestantism in an Age of Science*, 82–85, 139–43; Holifield, *Gentlemen Theologians*, chap. 4; Hovenkamp, *Science and Religion in America*, 41–56; Sidney E. Mead, *Nathaniel W. Taylor, 1786–1858: A Connecticut Liberal* (Hamden, CT: Archon Books, 1967); Conrad Wright, *The Beginnings of Unitarianism in America* (Boston: Beacon, 1954) 135–60.

[5] See, e.g., William Ellery Channing, "Evidences of Christianity, Parts I and II" and "Evidences of Revealed Religion," in *The Works of William E. Channing* (Boston: American Unitarian Association, 1888) 188–220, 220–32; Andrews Norton, *The Evidences of the Genuineness of the Gospels*, vol. 1 (Boston: American Stationer's Company, John B. Russell, 1837) vols. 2–3 (Cambridge, MA: John Owen, 1844); idem, *Internal Evidences of the Genuineness of the Gospels* (Boston: Little, Brown, 1855); Archibald Alexander, *Evidences of the Authenticity, Inspiration, and Canonical Authority of the Holy Scriptures* (Philadelphia: Presbyterian Board of Publication, 1836); idem, *The Canon of the Old and New Testaments Ascertained* (Philadelphia: Presbyterian Board of Publication, 1851); A. A. Hodge, *The Confession of Faith: A Handbook of Christian Doctrine Expounding the Westminster Confession [1867]* (London: Banner of Truth Trust, 1961). On Charles Hodge's presentation of natural theology and view of inspiration, see his *Systematic Theology* (Grand Rapids: Eerdmans, 1975) vol. 1, chaps. 1–2. The Princetonian combination of scholastic and Enlightenment rationalisms is noted in Jack B. Rogers and Donald W. McKim, *The Authority and Interpretation of the Bible: An Historical Approach* (San Francisco: Harper and Row, 1979) chaps. 4–5, with helpful notes; and in Ernest Sandeen, *The Roots of Fundamentalism: British and American Millenarianism, 1800–1930* (Chicago: University of Chicago Press, 1970) chap. 5.

formulas and to loosen the tie between intellectual assent and experimental (experiential) piety.

How pervasive these tendencies were at any given time and place does not need to be gauged here. Bushnell, at least, was alarmed by what he saw of them in evangelical and Unitarian religion.[6] To be sure, a preoccupation with revelation as information cannot be credited to apologetics alone. But Bushnell was of the opinion that apologetics had worked its will on doctrinal theology and that both were tainted by "rationalism."

If forced to choose between the customary apologetical strategy and a dogmatism that closed itself off from modern thought, Bushnell would doubtless have selected apologetics. Indeed, it was perhaps for this very reason that he complained so vigorously against a misguided and ineffectual defense of revealed religion. In *Nature and the Supernatural*, for example, he insists that "modern Christianity" has yielded "to the dominating ideas and fashions of the new religion, science, or supposed science of nature." The result is "a kind of revised Christianity . . . set up in the plane, saturated with the spirit, and even, where it is not suspected, compounded of the matter, of the science."[7] Conceding that "modern advances in science" brought about the turn from "supernatural evidences to natural evidences," he nevertheless concludes that "the evil in our present stage of thought, is that natural theology has the whole ground to itself, and the God established, is not a being who meets the conditions of Christianity at all."[8] The correct view arises when "the two worlds of evidences are seen to be complementary"—so long as priority is given to the "self-evidencing tokens" of the God revealed in the Bible and in the church.[9]

An even more striking statement of his view, however, appears in a letter written to his wife: "We are trying, and have been for centuries, to hold Christianity up in the lap of logic, reason, science, and the natural understanding, and the poor thing dwindles,—inconsequent, impotent, a shadow that has lost out the substance. The question now is whether it can live." Weary of "arguments, replies, ingenuities," Bushnell contends that the only hope of saving Christianity is "to see the possibility of revelation or its credibility in the present living fact."[10]

[6] See, e.g., Horace Bushnell, *God in Christ*, 99–101, 268–75; idem, *Christ in Theology* (Hartford: Brown and Parsons, 1851) 335; idem, "The Immediate Knowledge of God," *Sermons on Living Subjects* (Centenary Edition; New York: Charles Scribner's Sons, 1903) 115–16.

[7] Horace Bushnell, *Nature and the Supernatural, as Together Constituting the One System of God* (2d ed.; New York: Charles Scribner's Sons, 1901) 505–6.

[8] Ibid., 506–7.

[9] Ibid., 508–9.

[10] Cheyney, *Life and Letters*, 359.

These statements do not represent a renunciation of the apologetical and doctrinal tasks themselves. On the contrary, it would be hard to find a more earnest apologist than Bushnell. The argument set forth in *Nature and the Supernatural* illustrates the kind of apologetics he preferred. In demonstrating that the natural realm of cause and effect combines with the supernatural realm of free agency (God, angels, and human beings) to form one grand scheme of divine providence, the final appeal is to internal evidence—the power of Christianity to address and transform the human condition. And if one grants his definition of doctrine, one must acknowledge that he was a zealous, although atypical, "doctrinal" theologian.

But inasmuch as Bushnell's criticisms of the status quo and his plans for reform depended on a reconception of the category of revelation, he plumbed a level as yet untouched by such earlier theological revisionists as Nathaniel W. Taylor and William Ellery Channing.[11] Phrases such as "supernatural evidences," "self-evidencing tokens," and "the present, living fact" refer to an experiential relationship with God, which is said to be an immediate knowledge, or an inspiration, or a divine inner light, or a spiritual manifestation within the soul. It is the presence of God, apprehended in the modality of feeling—purity of heart, sentiment, love, faith.[12]

These references obviously betray his connections with the experimental religion of evangelical Protestantism and with the tide of nineteenth-century sentimentalism. But if his emphasis on a religion of the heart has its parallels in revivalistic enthusiasm, and if his insistence that spirituality is formative of moral character has its parallels in the didacticism of middle-class American culture, there is one other aspect of his thought that cannot be accounted for in such terms. For Bushnell, feeling is a structure of human selfhood, the locus of self-identity. Just as every person has a self-feeling that is intuitive and direct, so the Christian will have, as an accompaniment and modification of self-feeling, a consciousness of a "certain otherness" that moves within.[13] No merely intellectual proofs will substitute for an inward "revelation" of God.

This experience of the presence of God constitutes the essence of Christianity as spirit and life rather than as assent to religious ideas or commitment to moral ideals.[14] And on the assumption that the essence

---

[11] Welch, *Protestant Thought*, 127.

[12] See, e.g., Bushnell's statements in *God in Christ*, 335–36; *Christ in Theology*, 65–67, 82–83, 336–40; *Nature and the Supernatural*, 518; "The Reason of Faith," and "Regeneration," in *Sermons for the New Life* (rev. ed.; New York: Charles Scribner's Sons, 1895) 87–105, 106–26.

[13] Bushnell, "The Immediate Knowledge of God," *Sermons on Living Subjects*, 119–20.

[14] This point is emphasized by Robert Baird, "Horace Bushnell: A Romantic Approach to the Nature of Theology," *Journal of Bible and Religion* 33 (1965) 229.

of Christianity is inseparable from revelation itself, Bushnell identifies "the aim and purpose of all God's works" to be a revelation, that is, a communication "to creatures of that which is their Life, the warmth, light, beauty, and truth of the divine nature."[15] This conception of revelation was the magnet, so to speak, around which all of his dealings with the Bible and with biblical studies were clustered. The image may be especially apt because Bushnell's theology was less a "system of thought" than a collection of elements arrayed within an energy field. In any case, revelation was at the center of the field, repelling some types of inquiry and attracting others.

One type that was repelled was the pursuit of external evidences for the genuineness of biblical revelation. In Bushnell's judgment, "revolving God's ideas, systematizing external cognitions derived from his works, investigating the historic evidences of Christ, his life, his doctrines" were intellectual exercises that, apart from religious experience, produced darkness rather than light.[16] This depreciation of externality, however, removed one of the chief incentives that Christians of his day had for scholarly study of the authorship, dating, background, and historicity of the biblical materials. This is not to say that such topics were of no concern to Bushnell or to others with similar views of the essence of Christianity. There were other incentives and imperatives for such scholarship, and now and again Bushnell responded to them. Nonetheless, these inquiries held for Bushnell none of the promise and little of the peril that they did for Moses Stuart, Andrews Norton, or even Charles Hodge. For this reason, but not for this reason alone, he turned to more "fundamental" problems. Among them was this: what does it mean to say that the Bible is a "revelation of God"?

The question was on his mind when in 1839, only six years after graduation from divinity school, Bushnell accepted an invitation to address the Andover Society of Inquiry. His speech on "Revelation" was written in haste and never prepared for publication. It was a programmatic statement nonetheless. It showed that he had already cast aside New England "rationalism" and had adopted the view of revelation that he would use thereafter. The "central topic" of the address is "the Bible or Christian revelation," with specific reference to how finite objects function as media for revealing the divine life. The word revelation is explained by reference to the phenomenon of interpersonal communication, which is viewed as a sharing of life experience. The inner experiences, or "truths," of intelligent beings are "separate, invisible, immaterial worlds" within consciousness.[17] Directly

---

[15] Horace Bushnell, ["Revelation"] (MS, Yale Divinity School Library); transcription in Steward, "Horace Bushnell and Contemporary Christian Education," 309.

[16] Bushnell, *God in Christ*, 303.

[17] Bushnell, "Revelation," 314.

accessible to self-consciousness alone, "they can be made known to others only through the medium of some thing which answers to a revelation."[18] Thus the "fundamental idea of revelation," that is, "revelation in general," is understood as that which "brings truth into outward exhibition or into some one of the forms of the senses."[19] Rooted in God's "publicity," Christian revelation is a species of this genus.[20] Just as human beings announce their inner thoughts and feelings by means of some outward exhibition of facial features, bodily movements, or sounds, so God exhibits the divine mind in the outward forms of nature, history, and biblical language.[21]

The epistemological character of this model is evident, and David L. Smith has rightly noted its similarities to discussions among the Scottish Common Sense philosophers who sought to account for knowledge of other selves.[22] The question of Bushnell's sources is, and may remain, moot. The platonic cast of the argument, for example, may be due to the Augustinian strain of Puritan piety, to Scottish Common Sense, to romantic idealism, or to any combination of the three. It is important to note, however, that this approach to the question of revelation is by no means a direct continuation of discussions within the Anglo-American schools of empiricism. The decision to liken divine revelation to dialogical communication represents a break with the eighteenth-century heritage at several key points.[23]

The break is manifest, first, in that the topic has been taken with new seriousness. To be sure, the stakes involved in disputes over revelation had never been trivial. But Bushnell, it seems, considers the ante to be far higher than his evangelical and Unitarian colleagues had ever suspected. At risk is not "merely" the legitimacy of traditional references to revelation but the meaningfulness of any references to it at all. Or, to change the metaphor, one could say that in the midst of the prolonged debate over reason and revelation, Bushnell moves the previous question. The decision about which criteria are to judge the credibility of an alleged revelation must be delayed until the intelligibility of the word itself has been ascertained.

Second, this model of revelation as dialogical communication reflects a newly heightened sensitivity to problems related to subjectivity and intersubjectivity. The model itself assumes that communication must bridge the separation between an I and a thou who are alien individualities. In preromantic thought this assumption had figured in discussions

---

[18] Ibid., 310.

[19] Ibid., 309-10.

[20] Ibid., 309.

[21] Ibid., 310, 312-13; Bushnell, *God in Christ*, 17–20.

[22] D. L. Smith, *Symbolism and Growth*, 18–22.

[23] See Hans-Georg Gadamer's discussion of Schleiermacher's hermeneutical theory under the polemical title "The Questionableness of Romantic Hermeneutics," in *Truth and Method* (New York: Seabury, 1975) 153–73.

about artistic communication. But Bushnell extends it to every communicative act, including divine revelation. The extension has some curious
results. It permits Bushnell to give voice to a notion common in older
evangelicalism but obscured by scholastic and moralistic theologies: revelation is the self-communication of God, or, to rephrase the point, God is
both the subject and the object of revelation. It also turns revelation into
a matter of art par excellence—a conception that Bushnell more than
any other nineteenth-century theologian sets out to exploit in his biblical
and doctrinal studies. The media of revelation, including the language of
the Bible, overcome the distance between the divine and the human by
means of an aesthetic bridge, and the bridge is made up of two spans,
expression and understanding, which are self-involving acts on the part
of both sender and receiver. This means, of course, that the subject matter of the communication can be apprehended only in and through the
communicative process itself.

Bushnell was anxious about many things—his career above all. But
in posing and answering the question of the meaning of revelation as he
did, he gives no sign of anxiety about the correctness or the ultimately
favorable outcome of this line of thought. He does make revelation no
less mysterious than dialogical communication, and in so doing he further complicates an already complicated category. But he also makes
revelation no more mysterious than dialogical communication. One may
continue, and Bushnell does, to speak of nature, history, and the Bible as
revelations of God, because and so long as one recognizes that the media
of revelation are inseparable from but not identical to their content.
They are symbols—outward, sensory forms of what is beyond the senses.

In brief, Bushnell bases the Christian religion on revelation and
views revelation as symbolic expression. The point is stated crisply in
God in Christ: the pre-eminent and principal truth of Christianity is
"the expression of God—God coming into expression, through histories
and rites, through an incarnation, and through language—in one syl-
lable, by the WORD."[24] Given this premise, the task of theology will be
to explain how biblical expressions communicate the truth of God's identity. This is to be a descriptive rather than a speculative enterprise,
designed to clarify the nature of the revelatory process.

The Andover address identified "two great and indispensable conditions" for any revelation.[25] The first was that "there must be forms provided which are fit to be the signs or outward bodies of truth."[26] The second was that those who receive the revelation must have the "intelligence"

---

[24] Bushnell, *God in Christ*, 74.
[25] Bushnell, "Revelation," 310.
[26] Ibid., 310–11.

to read the forms and "to ascend" into the truth they communicate.[27] Each condition became a line of inquiry that Bushnell pursued in his later work. The first led to a study of biblical language; the second, to a study of biblical interpretation.

[27] Ibid., 311.

III

THE BIBLE AS POETRY

"The scriptures will be more studied than they have been and in a different manner—not as a magazine of propositions and mere dialectic entities, but as inspirations and poetic forms of life; requiring, also, divine inbreathings and exaltations in us, that we may ascend into their meaning."[1] This is what Bushnell predicted, or hoped, would result from his investigations into the nature of language. The comment makes it plain that Bushnell, the preacher and theologian, did intend to contribute to biblical scholarship, and the contribution he had in mind was nothing less than a total reorientation of the field: a "different manner" of study, which would focus on language and hermeneutics. It would begin with a general theory of language and conclude with a general theory of interpretation suitable for understanding the "poetic forms of life" in the Bible.

The problem of using language as an effective tool for communication had bothered Bushnell on a personal as well as a professional level since his college days. Recalling his life as a country boy at Yale, he wrote: "I had no language, and if I chanced to have an idea, nothing came to give it expression. The problem was, in fact, from that point onward, how to get a language, and where."[2] For a time he chose to copy the style of speaking and thinking found in Paley—exemplar of the didactic Enlightenment.[3] But his inability to give, or even to find, an intellectually satisfactory account of the articles of faith left him confused and skeptical. And since only the religious experiences of his "heart" were compelling enough to dissolve his doubts, he early on came to an interest in exploring the relationship between language and experience.[4]

---

[1] Bushnell, *God in Christ*, 93.

[2] Cheyney, *Life and Letters*, 208.

[3] Ibid., 208–9. Although marked by independent judgment, some of Bushnell's earliest works clearly show that he had appropriated not only the literary style but also the fundamental premises of the New Haven school; see "Natural Science and Moral Philosophy" and "There is a Moral Governor" (MSS, Yale Divinity School Library).

[4] In the account of his conversion it is reported that he came to hold the doctrine of the Trinity because of the promptings of his heart (Cheyney, *Life and Letters*, 55–60; see also Horace Bushnell, "The Dissolving of Doubts," *Sermons on Living Subjects*, 166–84). On his reading of Coleridge, see Cheyney (*Life and Letters*, 208–9) and the recollection

Some of the findings of that examination appeared in the Andover address "Revelation," for the viewpoint developed there depended on ideas taught by Gibbs and Coleridge. Yet it was not until 1849, a decade later, that Bushnell published an account of his theory of language. This report, "A Preliminary Dissertation on the Nature of Language as related to Thought and Spirit," was composed as the preface to *God in Christ*, a collection of lectures that had been delivered in 1848 at Yale, Harvard, and Andover.[5] Despite his disclaimer, the lectures were designed, in part at least, to break the deadlock beween Calvinism and Unitarianism by liberating both parties from the bonds of dogmatism.[6] This goal, he believed, could be attained if theologians would abandon their faulty assumptions about the language of religion. Scornful of proof-texts, literalism, and logical systematizing, he wished to show that a new approach to the Bible cleared the way for theological reform—an instrumental theory of the Trinity, a moral influence theory of the atonement, and an inversion of the relationship between the head (dogma) and the heart (the spirit). In light of the clamor his addresses had aroused, he decided that in publishing them he should explain in advance the principles on which his views were based.

The "Preliminary Dissertation" is notable in at least two respects: its placement and its content. Its placement signified that the meaningfulness of religious language was to be considered a root problem. That theology in general and biblical studies in particular could not avoid the question was a well-known and accepted fact of life. But American scholars were hardly prepared to hear that an investigation of "the significatory power, or the power of words and the capacity of words, taken as vehicles of thought and of spiritual truth" was an indispensable propaedeutic for any future theology.[7] Others labored and were laboring to stanch the wounds of the body of divinity; Bushnell urged that they be cauterized. In so doing he knowingly identified his work with that of Coleridge and unknowingly paralleled that of Schleiermacher.[8]

(p. 499) of J. H. Twichell: "I have often heard him say that he was more indebted to Coleridge than to any extra-Scriptural author."

5 Bushnell's *God in Christ* contains, in addition to the "Preliminary Dissertation," the following: "Concio ad Clerum: A Discourse on the Divinity of Christ: delivered at the Annual Commencement of Yale College, August 15, 1848"; "A Discourse on the Atonement, delivered before the Divinity School in Harvard University, July 9, 1848"; "A Discourse on Dogma and Spirit; or the True Reviving of Religion; delivered before the Porter Rhetorical Society, at Andover, September, 1848."

6 The disclaimer is given on p. 101 of *God in Christ*: "I have no thought, in the discussion that follows, or in the views maintained, of proposing any composition, or compromise, with the Unitarians. I have no confidence in any organic and combined effort of pacification between us. If we are ever re-united, it will be by a gradual and natural process, working in individual minds."

7 Ibid., 12.

8 See n. 4 above. Cherry (*Nature and Religious Imagination*, chap. 6) provides a succinct summary of Bushnell's indebtedness to Coleridge. Bushnell made explicit reference only to

The language theory itself cut against the grain of evangelical and Unitarian thought. As Donald Crosby has shown, discussions of language among religious scholars had in the main moved within the context of Lockean, Common Sense philosophy, and both the orthodox and the Unitarians shared a common commitment to "logical method as the norm of language."[9] On this view, "language can be the precise instrument of thought when words are carefully defined abstractions employed according to the rigorous logical method patterned after mathematics.[10] Bushnell, however, spoke on behalf of a rival school of opinion which held that figurative speech was the norm for linguistic usage. A passage in *Christ in Theology* encapsulates what he saw as the main point of contention:

> Reducing the truth of scripture into forms of abstract statement, under figures so effectually staled by time and familiarity that they seem, instead, to be literal and exact names of the ideas intended, it calls the product certainty; not perceiving that the appearance of certainty in which it rejoices is produced by simply doubling the uncertainty; that is, by having still on hand all the original uncertainty, and having it hidden from its own discovery. It supposes that generalities are most definite, because poetic form and figure are less palpable in them; whereas, the language that is most palpably figurative is generally more determinate and clear, and, as a matter of fact, far less frequently misunderstood than that of abstractive propositions.[11]

In pleading this case in the "Preliminary Dissertation," Bushnell developed a line of argument distinctively his own, although he frequently appealed to the research of scholars oriented to romanticism and idealism over against those oriented to British empirical thought.[12] The position established here became the base of operations for all his later work, and there is good reason to agree with the judgment of Mary Bushnell Cheney, his daughter and first biographer: *"Here . . . is the key to Horace Bushnell,* to the whole scheme of his thought, to that peculiar manner of expression which marked his individuality—in a

---

Schleiermacher's study of the doctrine of the Trinity ("On the Discrepancy between the Sabellian and Athanasian Method of Representing the Doctrine of the Trinity, translated with notes," by Moses Stuart, in the *American Biblical Repository* 5 [1835] 265–353, and 6 [1835] 1–116). Schleiermacher had earlier opened new paths in both hermeneutics and systematic theology by his reconception of the relationship between language and thought; see, e.g., Friedrich D. E. Schleiermacher, *Hermeneutics: The Handwritten Manuscripts* (ed. Heinze Kimmerle; trans. James O. Duke and Jack Forstman; Missoula, MT: Scholars Press, 1977) and idem, *The Christian Faith* (trans. H. R. Mackintosh and J. S. Stewart; Edinburgh: T & T Clark, 1928; reprinted, Philadelphia: Fortress, 1976) §§15–19.

9 Crosby, *Bushnell's Theory of Language*, 80–96.

10 Ibid., 79.

11 Bushnell, *Christ in Theology*, 42.

12 Crosby, *Bushnell's Theory of Language*, chap. 1.

word, to the man."[13] It is certainly the key to the different manner of biblical study he advocated. The recommendation to study biblical language as "inspirations and poetic forms of life" is rooted in the conviction that religious language is a symbolic expression of experience.

The "Preliminary Dissertation" was not a full investigation of language, but an inquiry into the nature and limits of linguistic communication. To be sure, this topic forced Bushnell to touch on a number of issues relevant to linguistics and to the philosophy of language.[14] But these were of interest only inasmuch as they had some bearing on how words functioned in communicating the life-experiences of consciousness. The chief finding may be briefly stated. Every language is composed of two tiers: the one a physical or literal department that provides "names for physical objects and appearances," the other an intellectual department of symbols "where physical objects and appearances are named as images of thought or spirit, and the words get their power, as words of thought, through the physical images received into them."[15]

This theory obviously takes words and combinations of words to be "pointers" that one person employs in order to direct another person to a given experience. But language in the two departments "points" differently. As names of sensory experiences that are, in principle, observable to all, words in the physical department point directly to some aspect or feature in the external world. Thus they bear a literal or "notational" meaning. If care is taken to correlate words and phenomena, these terms may be honed into sharp and precise equivalents of truth—a task Bushnell believed the sciences could undertake with considerable success.[16]

But inner experiences of consciousness—thoughts, sentiments, states of religious awareness—present themselves in no intersubjectively perceptible form, or indeed in any sensory form at all. Consequently, communication must take place by a method of indirection: "The soul flies to whatever implements it can find in the visible world, calling them to be

---

[13] Cheyney, *Life and Letters*, 203.

[14] E.g., he touched on the origin of language, the relationship between sound and meaning, and grammatical structure.

[15] Bushnell, *God in Christ*, 38–39. There is, however, an exception: "There is only a single class of intellectual words that can be said to have a perfectly determinate significance, viz., those which relate to what are called necessary ideas. They are such as time, space, cause, truth, right, arithmetical numbers, and geometrical figures. Here the names applied, are settled into a perfectly determinate meaning, not by any peculiar virtue in *them*, but by reason of the absolute exactness of the ideas themselves" (p. 46).

[16] Bushnell holds, however, that even terms in the physical department of language are inherently indeterminate in the sense that they name genera or classes of sensations (*God in Christ*, 43–44), and hence science must labor for precision. See *God in Christ*, 78–79, 308–9; idem, *Christ in Theology*, 29–32; idem, "Our Gospel a Gift to the Imagination," *Building Eras in Religion*, 271–72; see also Crosby, *Bushnell's Theory of Language*, 174 and n. 93.

interpreters."[17] Due to an "analogy" between things in the outer world of sense and things of the mind and spirit, words that refer to sensory appearances are transferred to the intellectual department, and there they find reemployment as signs indicating that inner experience is "like" some sensory experience that can be known and named.[18] Thus words in the intellectual department of language are no longer denotative but expressive. One looks in vain for a straightforward definition of this second-level meaning. Bushnell variously calls it figurative, imagic, analogical, metaphorical, or symbolic. He does make it clear that there is some correspondence between the two levels, for the symbolic meaning can be suggested only through literality. Beyond this, however, nothing more can be said. "On the one hand, is form; on the other, is the formless. The former represents and is somehow fellow to the other; how, we cannot discover."[19]

In Bushnell's judgment, then, all words and word patterns arise from the association of sounds with sensible objects and their interactions. Linguistic conventions developed over centuries of use have led persons to forget that they express their thoughts, feelings, and religion by terms whose meanings are derived from but not identical to sensory images. One result of such forgetfulness is that communication is often hampered by the misuse and misunderstanding of language. Another is that persons aspire to a standard of exactitude that intellectual discourse can never attain because it is incapable of complete determinacy of meaning. The transfer of meaning that occurs when word usage shifts from ostensive reference to symbolic expressivity defies precise calculation. Moreover, in imputing a sensory form to what is formless, symbols always affirm something false as well as something analogically true. The measures taken to overcome all ambiguity, for example, definitions, formulas ("little forms"), and logic, are not only ineffectual but dangerous, for in the process of manipulating the word images one is likely to miss their symbolic import altogether. Symbolic indeterminacy cannot be escaped.[20]

Nor should it be. It is precisely because symbols partake of, yet point beyond, their literal meaning that they can serve as the organon and vehicle of thought, and Bushnell insists that they are quite adequate for

---

[17] Bushnell, *God in Christ*, 23.

[18] Bushnell contends that the divine Logos present in the outer and inner worlds establishes the analogical connection between the two spheres (*God in Christ*, 21–22, 29–30, 38–40, 43). The discussion in Crosby (*Bushnell's Theory of Language*, 19–23) is a helpful account.

[19] Bushnell, *God in Christ*, 43.

[20] Ibid., 44–46, 48–49, 77–78; idem, *Christ in Theology*, 51. The principle is fundamental for Bushnell's criticism of his contemporaries and for his plan for theological reform.

the purpose of communication when they are rightly handled.[21] One must become sensitive to the "latent element" of sensory form contained in every word, for this gives the word its metaphoric reach.[22] The linguistic virtuosity of a great poet, for example, demonstrates how symbols can be used with power. In the poet the instinct that first created language is kindled into perspicuity—a genius for discerning analogies between mind and matter and for casting up symbols in order to express the world of inner experience.

The literary artist also shows how expressive language, as imprecise as it is, can be employed so that it is able to "mend its own deficiencies."[23] Since one symbol gives only a partial, and therefore misleading, glimpse of a truth, it is necessary to "multiply words or figures and thus to present the subject on opposite sides or many sides."[24] The most "rounded view of any truth" emerges from the interaction of many forms: "Thus, as form battles form, and one form neutralizes another, all the insufficiencies of words are filled out, the contrarieties liquidated, and the mind settles into a full and just apprehension of the pure spiritual truth."[25] The principle is that contradictions at one level are complementary at another level.

The "pure spiritual truth" communicated by literary artists or any serious thinkers is the result of a donation given in and by expressive symbols. The signifier with its literal signification is the only means of access to what is signified, but what is signified is a second-level order of meaning.

Symbols do not, however, "convey" or "carry over" contents of consciousness from one person to another. They are only " . . . hints or images, held up before the mind of another, to put *him* on generating or reproducing the same thought; which he can do only as he has the same personal contents, or the generative power, out of which to bring the thought required."[26] If the signifier is a symbol, the signified is the change that is brought about in the consciousness of the listener or reader. As David Smith aptly puts it, "A truth of expression is ultimately a state of the soul, a quality of life, whose 'truth' is its self-evidencing value as a mode of experience. It is a 'truth' that closely resembles 'beauty' on the subjectivist account—i.e. it is not a property of an object or statement but a quality of our response to a form."[27] Symbolic expression, then, is an act of evocation. The language of texts engages the subjectivity of the readers and beckons them toward a new world of inner experience.

21 Bushnell, *Christ in Theology*, 33, 58–59.
22 Bushnell, *God in Christ*, 24–25, 50–52, 80; idem, *Christ in Theology*, 48–49.
23 Ibid., 55.
24 Ibid.
25 Ibid.
26 Bushnell, *God in Christ*, 46.
27 D.L. Smith, *Symbolism and Growth*, 118.

Bushnell's "different manner" of biblical study is founded on this view of language. Since "religion has a natural and profound alliance with poetry,"[28] the language of the Bible, like all religious language, is to be read as symbolic expression. Consequently, biblical study will be tailored more along the lines of a literary criticism than of historical or philosophical analysis. This is true, Bushnell contends, whether the biblical texts are considered individually as the works of specific speakers and authors or collectively as a single work expressive of the divine author. Indeed, he assumes that they are to be regarded in both ways simultaneously. Each text is at once the poetic articulation of human authors setting forth their experiential apprehension of religious truth and the poetic articulation of God, the author of the authors, setting forth through the experiences and words of humans the truth of the divine nature.

In commending this approach Bushnell repeatedly draws attention to quasi-aesthetic features of the Bible. He maintains that the language used by speakers in the biblical texts and by the authors of the biblical texts is more akin to that of poetry than to that of the market place or the academy. For example, "the teachings of Christ are mere utterances of truth, not argumentations over it. He gives it forth in living symbols, without definition, without *proving* it, ever, as the logicians speak."[29] And Paul, who is to many a master dialectician and systematician, is to Bushnell a "seer." The "dialectic form" and "deductive manner" of his presentation are carried over from his "old theologic discipline, previous to his conversion." In this respect his use of language, like that of every author, betrays the formative influences of his personal history. But those who read "with true insight" will realize that "under the form of ratiocination, he is not so much theologizing as flaming in holy inspirations of truth." He offers no "theologic system"; his epistles are always directed to specific occasions, situations, and issues. His "illatives and deductive propositions" do not proceed by logic but like a "stream of Christian fire." The study of Pauline literature must therefore be of the sort attuned to "a prophesying of the spirit" rather than to "a Socratic lecture."[30]

This approach allows Bushnell to acknowledge that the biblical canon is a collection of units representing individual, diverse, limited, and even contradictory viewpoints. Its "law-givers, heroes, poets, historians, prophets, and preachers and doers of righteousness" reflect different ages, characters, and modes of thought.[31] The life and teachings of Jesus receive manifold presentation. The "four, some say five, distinct writers" of the

---

28 Bushnell, *God in Christ*, 74.
29 Ibid., 75.
30 Ibid., 75–76.
31 Ibid., 70.

epistles offer "each his own view of the doctrine of salvation and the Christian life, (views so unlike or antagonistical that many have regarded them as being quite irreconcileable)—Paul, the dialectic, commonly so-called; John, the mystic; James, the moralizer; Peter, the homiletic; and perhaps a fifth in the epistle to the Hebrews, who is a Christian templar and a Hebraizer."[32]

This sort of taxonomy of New Testament literature was by no means exceptional for the day. Bushnell's equivocal stand on the authorship of Hebrews, for example, hardly amounts to a decisive judgment on a matter of some debate among New England scholars.[33] At one level it is hardly more than an evasive tactic he employed frequently in his ministry. At another level, however, it illustrates a point worthy of comment. His equivocation reflects a relative indifference to the question of authorship, which is itself hermeneutically significant. For Bushnell the power of a text to communicate its truth is vested in the poetic forms of life contained in it. Since knowledge of authorship neither determines nor confirms the truth of the text, there is no need to identify the author in order to understand what is written. Reading centers on the text itself, which on this view must be granted a degree of literary autonomy.

To be sure, this is a qualified autonomy, compromised on the one hand by a tendency to accept traditional judgments about biblical history and on the other hand by the insistence that communication involves a production and reproduction of personal experience. Nonetheless, Bushnell's view of language does not demand that one shift from the text to a dogmatic grid or to a reconstructed history in order to unlock its meaning. And even the limits imposed on textual autonomy are applied with some caution. Bushnell is open to untraditional judgments about biblical literature and he shows no interest in grasping an authorial intention apart from linguistic expressions.

Bushnell advocated taking the Bible as an aesthetic object, expressive of God. "In the form of political and religious annals, the biographies of distinguished saints, the teachings of the prophets, the incarnate life and death of the Word made flesh," the reader meets outward forms that give hints and images of divinity.[34] The work of Michaelis, Lowth, Herder, and others had alerted some New England scholars to the significance of poetry and poetic-like passages in the Bible.[35] Bushnell readily admits that literal terminology appears in portions of the canon that are historical and didactic, but "even these have their prose largely sprinkled with poetry." The parables, for example, are didactic; yet they are in

---

32 Ibid.
33 Brown, *Biblical Criticism in America*, 91.
34 Bushnell, *Christ in Theology*, 82.
35 Crosby, *Bushnell's Theory of Language*, 134–35.

fact only "metaphors drawn out."[36] And the arguments in the epistles turn on "figures of speech, such as law, circumcision, heart, grace, kingdom, life, motions of sin, liberty, flesh."[37] Even the historical narratives are to be read as poetic forms, for "history itself, in fact, is but a kind of figure, having its greatest value, not in what it is, but in what it signifies."[38] And what it signifies is "an evolution of expression of God and man in their own nature and character"—a subject matter that transcends the ostensive reference of historical narration.[39]

Bushnell ordinarily accepted the historicity of the events recorded in the Bible without question. Only on occasion is any other alternative considered. He notes and permits the scholarly viewpoint that regards the "primeval history" in the early chapters of Genesis as "mythic" rather than "factual." And he argues that the gospels are to be considered as substantially accurate, even though they may not be correct in every detail.[40] Such judgments—and Bushnell too often hedges on them—are influenced by historical, literary, and quite obviously, theological considerations. But in claiming that biblical history, no less than biblical poetry and paraenesis, is a gallery of pictorial symbols expressive of religious truth, Bushnell has no need to confirm or to reconstruct the actual events in order to understand the Bible. The significatory power of the texts depends on their language, not on the history that lies behind the language. Taken as the works of human authors, biblical writings are symbolic expressions of experiences (thoughts, feelings, religious insights and inspirations) that modern historians may or may not credit as fact. Taken as the work of a divine author, they are symbols that, in the form of history, poetry, myth, or whatever, express God's disposition toward humanity.

In Bushnell's opinion, the diverse "poetic forms" found within the pages of the Bible constitute an expressive whole. This is an opinion that he explains but does not bother to substantiate. The explanation is an appeal to other examples of great literature. Just as the "truth" to be communicated by a "difficult," that is, profound, author like Goethe requires an ensemble of symbols, so a revelation of God will patently make use of a wide diversity of materials. "There is no book in the world," Bushnell claims, "that contains so many repugnances, or antagonistic forms of assertion, as the

---

[36] Bushnell, "Our Gospel a Gift," *Building Eras in Religion*, 264.

[37] Ibid.

[38] Ibid.

[39] Bushnell, *God in Christ*, 75. See idem, "Revelation," 310: "Revelation is further distinguished from history or a narrative of facts. A revelation may be made by means of facts and narratives, or through them, but it will be yet no more identical with them than are the letters in which truth is written with truth itself."

[40] See chap. 7 below; on the creation story, see Bushnell, "Our Gospel A Gift," *Building Eras in Religion*, 257–58.

Bible."[41] "The great mystery of godliness" requires "a whole universe of rite, symbol, incarnation, historic breathings, and poetic fires, to give it expression—in a word, just what it now has."[42] Through the interplay and conflict of manifold terms, the Bible communicates one truth, the character of God.

[41] Bushnell, *God in Christ*, 69.
[42] Ibid., 71.

IV

THE ASCENT INTO MEANING

On the basis of his theory of language, Bushnell believed he could show that a Bible composed of poetic forms of life was a vehicle fit for the revelation of divine truth. There remained, however, one other condition for the possibility of any revelation—those who receive it must have the "intelligence" or, as he also put it, the "understanding" to read the symbols rightly and to ascend into their meanings. His reflections on this condition led him to investigate the nature of biblical interpretation, which is taken to be an effort to understand linguistic expressions. He duly noted that only beings at a level of intelligence above that of mere animals can express and understand symbolic discourse.[1] But beyond this he had to deal with the proper exercise of intelligence upon symbols. "Perhaps it is one of the highest errands of our life," he wrote, "to learn the method of finding truths in their forms."[2]

It is unfortunate that Bushnell did not write a preliminary dissertation on hermeneutics or a handbook of exegetical method. In the absence of such a statement, his account of the interpretive task must be pieced together from comments and illustrations scattered throughout his work. What emerges from his works is a proposal that may be termed a hermeneutics of aesthetic engagement, that is, a conception of the interpretive task which takes artistic communication as its paradigm. It was a new departure in biblical hermeneutics to approach biblical language as artistic symbols and to liken biblical understanding to artistic responsiveness. And it spelled a revised estimate of the nature and goal of interpretation theory, subordinating the typically eighteenth-century interest in the specification of philological rules to an interest in the description of linguistic understanding. Bushnell does offer guidelines for interpretation, often drawing upon observations about literary criticism. But these do not amount to a method in the sense of a step-by-step procedure that insures objectively valid results. Perhaps nothing other could be expected from an advocate of a "divinatory method." In any case his reflections on biblical hermeneutics focus more on how understanding occurs than on

---

[1] Bushnell, "Revelation," 311; idem. "Our Gospel A Gift," *Building Eras in Religion,* 252.

[2] Bushnell, *Christ in Theology,* 31.

what rules govern judgments about competing interpretations.

According to Bushnell, a proper reading of the Bible begins with the recognition that symbolic language is expressive rather than notational. "The great principle to be adopted is that all the presentations we meet of truth or spiritual doctrine in the Bible lie in figures, and there must be studied."[3] This principle obviously arises directly from his language theory, and it reflects his dedication to the proposition that the Bible is to be interpreted like any other book, for, as he observes, "all mental thought and moral truth lies in the same condition."[4] This commitment was part of the legacy of the Enlightenment, and it was widely, if by no means universally, shared by New England biblical scholars. Yet inasmuch as this particular principle repudiated every literalism, it was a challenge to dogmatic, grammatical, and historical critics alike.

To this principle is joined another. The "fact-forms" or "symbols" of the Bible are addressed to the imaginative rather than the "notational understanding" or speculative reason.[5] The epistemological distinctions implied here are blurred in Bushnell's work—perhaps a symptom of his disdain for technical precision, certainly a symptom of his attenuated appropriation of Coleridge. At any rate, Bushnell ceaselessly repeats that symbols are understood by an act of the imagination and that biblical interpretation is a matter of "imaginative insight" or "imaginative reason."[6] By the "imagination," he means a power of intelligence that "distinguishes truths in their images, and seizes hold of images for the expression of truths."[7] The notational understanding, it would seem, is the faculty of mind that acts to identify, associate, and reflect upon ideas derived from sensory experiences taken in and of themselves. Speculative reason deals with abstract, formal concepts and their necessary, that is, analytic, interrelations. But the imagination detects in phenomena "truths" that effect a change within the subject who views them. It is both an inlet to and an outlet of states of inner awareness, and for this reason Bushnell associates it closely with "aesthetic perception," sentiment, feeling, and faith.

In all likelihood Bushnell thought of imagination as one of the "faculties" of mind. He does not develop a faculty psychology, however, and his remarks on the imagination almost always deal with it as a mode of apprehension distinct from conceptualization. In the interpretive task, the imagination is the organ of receptivity.[8] It attends to symbolic displays by a

---

3 Bushnell, "Revelation," 324; see also idem, *Christ in Theology*, 15.

4 Bushnell, "Revelation," 235.

5 Bushnell, *God in Christ*, 102, 105, 111; idem, *Christ in Theology*, 92; idem, "Our Gospel A Gift," *Building Eras in Religion*, 249–50, 252, 263, 272, 724–25.

6 Crosby, *Bushnell's Theory of Language*, 41–45.

7 Bushnell, "Our Gospel A Gift," *Building Eras in Religion*, 265.

8 Ibid., 266; idem, *Christ in Theology*, 16–17, 34; Cherry, *Nature and Religious Imagination*, 173–74.

"simple inspection," absorbing what is expressed by absorbing itself in the expressions. It apprehends meanings on the face of things, just as one grasps the dispositions of friends in their facial features or just as one grasps the message of artists in their paintings.[9] Thus the founding moment of interpretation is an encounter between text and interpreter in which the text is the active partner. At issue is not what the interpreter can say about or do with the symbols, but what the symbols say and do to the interpreter. By contemplating language as an expression, the reader receives sensory impressions that bear nonsensory meanings.

Bushnell complains that contemporary biblical interpreters typically disregard both principles. "They assume," he charges, "that there is a literal terminology in religion as well as a figurative, . . . and then it is only part of the same mistake to accept words, not as signs and images, but as absolute measures and equivalents of truth."[10] They mistake biblical symbols for notations of clear and distinct ideas, and subject them to an "overly wise and perversely ingenious industry of the head," which deduces, inducts, and spins out logically consistent propositions.[11] Bushnell is scornful of this "intensely dogmatizing habit," which busies itself "*about* and *upon* truth, as a dead body offered to the scalpels of logic," and he urges interpreters to approach the "truth as set before us in living expression."[12] What may be taken as his final verdict is harsh:

> Our theologic method in New England has been essentially rationalistic; though not exactly in the German sense. The possibility of reasoning out religion, though denied in words, has yet been tacitly assumed. Not allowing ourselves to be rationalists *over* the scriptures, we have yet been as active and confident rationalists *under* them, as it was possible to be—assuming, always, that they address their contents to the systematic, speculative reason.[13]

His antidote to rationalism is imaginative receptivity.

The aesthetic character of this proposal for interpretation is evident in the few practical hints that are offered to readers of the Bible. They are advised to identify whether an author "takes up some given word or figure, and makes it a law to his thinking."[14] Taken as an analogy, the literal meaning of the word—which Bushnell often discovers by tracing its etymology—directs the mind toward a nonsensory meaning, and by referring the other words of the text to this dominant image one may come to glimpse the truth to be communicated. But Bushnell makes it plain that he has little respect for such "easy" or "clear" authors. The

9 Bushnell, *Christ in Theology*, 16–17.
10 Bushnell, *God in Christ*, 40.
11 Bushnell, *Christ in Theology*, 92.
12 Ibid., 32.
13 Bushnell, *God in Christ*, 92.
14 Ibid., 65.

simplicity of their style indicates either that they are dealing with a very
simple truth or that they are dealing with a truth in very simplistic
terms.

Of greater worth are the "difficult" writers who broach profound
truths in a serious manner. These authors call upon a multitude of symbols in order to circle and offer a cross-view of the truth, and only a
comprehensive reading can do justice to their works. "We are to pass
round accordingly with him [the author], take up all his symbols, catch a
view of him here, and another there, use one thing to qualify and interpret another, and the other to shed light upon that, and, by a process of
this kind, endeavor to comprehend his antagonisms, and settle into a
complete view of his meaning."[15] Bushnell cites with approval Ecker-
mann's rejoinder to critics who grumble about the "inconsistencies" in
Goethe's account of the nature of poetry: "these seeming contradictions
are, in fact, only successive presentations of single sides of a truth,
which, by their union, manifest completely to us its existence, and guide
us to a perception of its nature."[16]

Evidently, reading the Bible should be no different from reading
Goethe. To the "mere wordsman" the profusion of tensive symbols in the
book of John, or in the Bible as a whole, seems intolerable. In despera-
tion, the orthodox "seize upon some one symbol as the real form of truth,
and compel all the others to submit to it"; the Unitarians "decoct the
whole mass of symbol and draw off the extract into pitchers of our
own."[17] By short-circuiting the interplay of literary symbols in these
ways, these interpreters miss the meaning of the texts altogether. The
wise critic will stay with the symbols, move with them as they recoil
against one another, yield to their impressions, and "gravitate inwardly,
towards that whole of truth, in which they coalesce."[18]

Crucial to this criticism, which is at once simple and comprehensive,
is the positioning of the interpreter vis-à-vis the text. Bushnell urges that
a generous amount of sympathy be extended to every serious author.[19]
This plea was not uncommon in preromantic hermeneutics; in romanticism, and in Bushnell, it becomes indispensable to the interpretive task.[20]
Sympathetic interpreters will be open and receptive to the impressions
coming from the text. They will refrain from any precipitate judgments

[15] Ibid., 67.
[16] Ibid., 68.
[17] Ibid., 69.
[18] Ibid., 71.
[19] Ibid., 89; idem, *Christ in Theology*, 65–66.
[20] See Frei, *Eclipse of Biblical Narrative*, 184–92; 242–45, 298, 305–6; and Richard
Palmer, *Hermeneutics: Interpretation Theory in Schleiermacher, Dilthey, Heidegger,
and Gadamer* (Northwestern University Studies in Phenomenology and Existential Philosophy; Evanston, IL: Northwestern University, 1969) 81–83, 87–97.

about it. They will offer the author the "indulgence" of presuming that the work is a many-sided unity. They will celebrate a multiplicity of antagonistic symbols. They will "feel out" the "pure truth" from the forms of expression.[21]

Why the proper attitude of the interpreter plays such a decisive role in Bushnell's theory of interpretation is not hard to fathom. His rendition of the hermeneutical circle must be cited as one reason: "Life is organic; and if there be life in his [an author's] work, it will be found not in some noun or verb that he uses, but in the organic whole of his creations. Hence it is clear that he must be apprehended in some sense, as a whole, before his full import can be received in paragraphs and sentences."[22] As an effort to communicate, a text is not a thing but a voice. The individuality of the author is invested in the individuality of the work, and the language that is shaped to express life experience bears the stamp not only of sensory forms but of "personal habit and character."[23] Every author "who can properly be called a living soul," Bushnell explains, uses words "with a significance and power breathed into them, which is wholly peculiar—whether it be in the rhythm, the collocations, the cadences, or the internal ideas, it may be impossible to guess."[24] In short, the irreducible particularity of personal life is embodied in the style of writing. Sympathy is required in order "to bring one into the inward life and sphere of the other."[25] By this means the interpreter may intuitively grasp the individuality that has molded language into a message, and thereby come "to reproduce him [the author] or his thought, that is, to make a realization of him."[26]

Implicit in this conception of the hermeneutical circle is the assumption that dialogical communication, which attempts to bridge the gulf between the I and the thou, depends on an underlying unity of spirit. Sympathy, then, is the state of intersubjective accord that acknowledges the individuality of the author within the universal connectedness of life. Individuality itself emerges at the intersection of a common nature and a particularized character; the individuality of a literary work emerges at the intersection of a common language and a particularized use of that language. Sympathy positions the interpreter within the intersection where individuality emerges.

It is clear that Bushnell's hermeneutics includes both grammatical and psychological "moments." He does not intend to disregard the kind of considerations that grammatico-historical critics bring to bear on texts

---

[21] See n. 19 above, and Bushnell, *Christ in Theology*, 47.
[22] Bushnell, *God in Christ*, 85.
[23] Ibid., 84.
[24] Ibid.
[25] Bushnell, *Christ in Theology*, 47.
[26] Bushnell, *God in Christ*, 34.

but to offer a corrective to their procedures. The determinations of meaning made by the grammarians, lexicographers, and historians may serve "as a guide to use, but never a limit upon use."[27] Beyond knowledge of the historical state of language is the knowledge, born of sympathetic insight, of the distinctive modification of the language that is wrought by creative thinkers. That there are no rules for such insight, that hermeneutics is an "art" rather than a science, Bushnell would have to admit. But this admission does not make him a hermeneutical enthusiast. Sympathy is to lead the interpreter not away from the *usus loquendi* but into it. Only a sympathetic interpreter can avoid imposing a meaning abstracted from word usage in other texts upon that in the individual text under investigation.

Despite the psychologizing thrust of Bushnell's comments about reproducing the inner experience of the author, he attempts to stop short of psychologism. He refuses to claim that interpreters could or should enter into the inward life of the author except through the expressions given in the text. He does not advocate reconstructing the process of creation that produced the text or explaining the text by "psychoanalysis" of the author. Sympathy, intuition, insight, divination—these are acts by which the interpreter makes an effort to understand that which an author has made an effort to express. Communication "succeeds" when effort meets effort at the text. At this point alone can the meaning of the text be determined.

In fact, however, the aim of interpretation is not so much the "determination" of meaning, that is, an act that the interpreter imposes upon the text, as it is an experience that the interpreter undergoes. Bushnell speaks of an ascent into meaning. Symbols do not transfer meaning from one person to another. They elicit a response, and it is this that is their meaning, subject matter, or truth: "What they [words] carry into our souls' feeling or perception, or awaken in it by expression, is their only truth, and that is a simple state of the soul itself."[28] The engagement between text and reader transforms the subjectivity of the interpreter.

By this account symbolic discourse is a "wondrous art by which some men are able to propitiate and assist the generative understanding of others, so as to draw them readily into higher realizations of truth."[29] No matter how stimulative the symbols may be, however, they must be matched by a willingness and an ability on the part of interpreters to set about producing the inner experience they suggest. As the willingness and ability of readers vary, so will the degree of understanding: "There will be different measures of understanding or misunderstanding, according to the capacity

[27] Ibid., 84.
[28] Bushnell, *Christ in Theology*, 17.
[29] Bushnell, *God in Christ*, 88.

or incapacity, the ingenuousness or moral obliquity of the receiving party—even if the communicating party offers only truth, in the best and freshest forms of expression the language provides."[30] In short, communication occurs when symbols powerful enough to engage the life of another meet a life powerful enough to be engaged by them.

Bushnell believed that his interpretive theory would befit "the second age of the church or society, the historical and critical age." Even though this reference to the ages of the church appears in the course of discussing the interpretation of creeds, it pertains equally well to biblical interpretation. In the first age, the forms of truth were equated with the truth itself. "But, in the second age, opinions become a subject of comparison, their laws are inquired after, their forms become plastic, and are seen to be melting into each other. Under contrary forms are found common truths, and one form is seen to be the complement of another,—all forms, we may almost say, the complement of all others."[31] Christ attained such comprehensiveness "in the native grandeur of his own spirit." Those living in the historical and critical age may gain an equally comprehensive view—but only "by a laborious criticism." It was just such a criticism that Bushnell sought to foster by means of his views of language and hermeneutics.

The fact of the matter is that the historical and critical age did not embrace this theory of interpretation. Like their European counterparts, who were often their mentors, American biblical interpreters were inclined to allow their judgments about the subject matter of the biblical texts to govern their interpretations of textual meaning. As Hans Frei has shown in *The Eclipse of Biblical Narrative*, the range of subject matter proposals was broad.[32] The common conception of meaning-as-reference permitted considerable disagreement about the referents—historical facts, ideas of doctrine or morality, modes of consciousness, or some combination of the three. Bushnell too, it has been noted, shared this preoccupation with subject matter, which he identified as an inner experience of consciousness. Yet in several respects his hermeneutics was singular.

First, although he refused to equate the language of the Bible with its subject matter, he also refused to separate them. The truth evoked by biblical symbols is neither to be gained nor explicated apart from the symbols. It is for this reason that Bushnell has no cause to search out the facts, ideas, or states of mind that lay behind the text in order to shed light on textual meaning. The attempt to probe behind the text is, in his judgment, "as if Moses, when he saw the burning bush, had fallen at once to speculating about the fire."[33] And it is for this reason, too, that

---

[30] Ibid., 46.
[31] Bushnell, "Christian Comprehensiveness," *Building Eras in Religion*, 391.
[32] Frei, *Eclipse of Biblical Narrative*, 255–66.
[33] Bushnell, *God in Christ*, 158.

he takes no interest in reconstructing the ideas or modes of consciousness that lay behind a literary work in order to translate their meaning into an abstract, nonsymbolic summary.

Second, explication and application merge in Bushnell's hermeneutics, and only the merger can be called "understanding." At this point he diverges from all his dogmatic and critical competitors and has at his disposal a resource to combat both dogmatism and historicism. Uncritical, grammatical, grammatico-historical, and historical interpretations result, each in its own way, in an explication of meaning that somehow stands over against the interpreter and awaits appropriation. Whether one accepts the ostensive reference of the texts as their truth or one seeks to apprehend the truth behind the ostensive reference, the outcome is the same: explicative meaning falls short of what Bushnell would call genuine understanding. When the biblical texts are taken as windows through which one glimpses a distant world of meaning, one must then overcome that distance by some post-hermeneutical move. For Bushnell, however, texts—insofar as they are understood—are mirrors by which a once-distant world of meaning is projected upon and within the life of the reader. Thus, his criticism of a "mere explication" of the life of Christ would apply to both uncritical and critical interpretations: "The Christian facts are stored in history, and are scarcely more significant to us than if they were stored in the moon."[34] To be "significant" for contemporary life, that is, to communicate the truth of God, the Bible must yield its meaning within the horizon of the present.

Taken as a whole, Bushnell's comments on biblical interpretation may be said to provide a sketch of a general theory of hermeneutics applicable to any literary text. The process of interpretation involves three essential elements or "moments"—symbol, imaginative receptivity, and ascent into meaning. Whatever is to be said of a special biblical hermeneutics must be consonant with this description of the interpretive experience. And Bushnell does consider the Bible, as the revelation of God, to be a special case.

Since Bushnell holds that every author deserves a sympathetic interpreter, he can maintain that "it ought not to be a hard necessity that a like sympathy to God is requisite to make a true doctrine of God, whether in the words of man or of Scripture, intelligible and clear to the mind."[35] It is evident, however, that "a like sympathy to God" is something more than the attitude of openness, tolerance, and sincerity which the interpreter grants any great author. In order to understand the Bible, one must come to it with "a pure and loving heart," "a delicate reverence," and "a generous

---

[34] Bushnell, "The Reason of Faith," *Sermons for the New Life*, 94.
[35] Bushnell, *Christ in Theology*, 65.

faith."[36] And since not even the "wondrous art" of a genius can move a reader "under the ribs of death,"[37] the expressions of God in the Bible cannot by themselves lift sinful humanity into their meaning. Bushnell therefore contends: "Mere revelation, or a word of truth that has gotten form in a language, has by itself no effectually quickening or regenerative power in character. It stands before the mind, glassing truth in a way to act upon it, but it can accomplish nothing save as another kind of power acting in the mind makes it impressible under and by the truth."[38] This other kind of power is "a large infusion of the divine spirit," "a supernatural light," which brings the interpreter "to know the meaning of things, and conform, with a divine facility, to that which is truest and best in them."[39]

It is by no means certain whether these appeals to faith and to divine illumination are indicative of the conservative or of the progressive streak in Bushnell's thought. The insertion of these traditional evangelical themes into his account turns reading the Bible into a very special hermeneutics indeed. Yet it is remarkable that he goes to such lengths to incorporate these themes into the framework of his distinctively "modern" (nineteenth-century) biblical hermeneutics oriented to literary studies. The elements constitutive of understanding—symbol, imagination, sympathetic receptivity, and ascent into meaning—remain intact, and everything that is said about faith and the inner witness of the spirit is fitted within this context.

To be sure, the fit is not altogether comfortable. It is not clear what love, reverence, and faith add to an already generous amount of sympathy, except an increased receptivity to the infusion of the spirit. And when Bushnell insists that the spirit does not come in or through the words of the text but acts immediately and internally on the mind of the interpreter, one cannot resist the temptation to say that his biblical hermeneutics must resort to a *deus ex machina*. If his theory had allowed for a sharp distinction between explication and application, or between meaning and truth, such appeals to faith and the spirit—however problematic they may be in and of themselves—might have been more intelligible. Indeed, he sometimes seems to represent a view not uncommon in the evangelical tradition: the same subject matter "glasses" before the minds of believers and nonbelievers alike, but only by the spirit does that subject matter receive "a power to enter and possess and lodge itself and be inwardly appropriated."[40] He can claim, for example, that "Christ is the mirror that glasses God's image before us, and the Spirit is the plastic form within, that

36 Ibid., 65–67.
37 Bushnell, *God in Christ*, 88.
38 Bushnell, "Inspiration by the Holy Spirit," *The Spirit in Man: Sermons and Selections* (New York: Charles Scribner's Sons, 1903) 22.
39 Bushnell, *Christ in Theology*, 336; see also idem, *God in Christ*, 308.
40 Bushnell, "Inspiration by the Holy Spirit," *Spirit in Man*, 22–23.

transfers and photographs the image."[41] In such cases the truth that is understood is "beyond form" only in the sense that it is an experience rather than a symbol of an experience. But there is nonetheless a congruence between the form and that which is experienced.

Bushnell can also claim, however, that the spirit heightens the "insight of faith," which is necessary for separating the symbolic "husk" from the pure truth and for gravitating toward a meaning around which a diversity of symbols coalesce. This would imply that the insightful interpreter has a somewhat different truth glassing before the mind than that available to anyone else. In pietism the theory of emphases had functioned in just this way.[42]

But Bushnell is ambiguous on the point. He does not explain exactly how a spiritual discernment of the "meaning and power" of symbols transcends a "natural judgment" about their meaning. Is it an existential appropriation of what has been naturally judged or a quite distinctive supernatural judgment that is existentially appropriated? A "sympathetic interpreter" in Bushnell's sense would perhaps be inclined toward the first alternative. Yet in merging explicative and applicative meanings Bushnell's interpretation theory never supplies a definitive answer.

[41] Bushnell, "The Completing of the Soul," *Sermons on Living Subjects*, 108.
[42] Dilthey, *Leben Schleiermachers*, 2:618–20; Frei, *Eclipse of Biblical Narrative*, 38–40.

V

THE AUTHORITY AND USE OF THE BIBLE

What Bushnell called a "different manner" of biblical study went hand in hand with new proposals regarding the authority and use of the Bible. The upshot was to be a theology in a new key. Given his views of the essence of Christianity, revelation, and biblical language, it should come as no surprise that he found the old key intolerable. Christianity is spiritual experience, not dogma; revelation is an act of solicitation, not the promulgation of information; religious language is symbolic, not notational. He disdained every attempt to construct "a speculative system of doctrine, drawn out in propositions . . . stated in terms that have finally obtained a literal and exact sense,"[1] and he chided his peers for their inordinate confidence in theologies, "little finite universes all, soap-bubble worlds rising by their own levity."[2] He lived in the hope that those who grew disillusioned with the makings, remakings, and "miscarriages" of theology might come to a fresh appreciation of symbolism and spiritual insight.[3]

His ardent denunciation of systematics at times made him sound like a theological Luddite and lent dignity to a cultured anti-intellectualism.[4] His true goal, however, was at once less extreme and more ambitious; he sought not to destroy but to rehabilitate the theological enterprise. His theory of religious language, in particular, was to be therapeutic.

> Showing that the advancement and the real amount of true theology depends, not on logical deductions and systematic solutions, but principally on the more cultivated and nicer apprehension of symbol, it may turn the industry of our teachers more in this direction, giving a more esthetic character to their studies and theories, and drawing them as much closer to the practical life of religion.[5]

[1] Bushnell, "Our Gospel A Gift," *Building Eras in Religion*, 268.

[2] Bushnell, *Christ in Theology*, 72.

[3] Ibid., 22.

[4] Foster, *Genetic History*, 406–7; Clebsch, *American Religious Thought*, 116. On nineteenth-century anti-intellectualism, see Richard Hofstadter, *Anti-Intellectualism in American Life* (New York: Random House, Vintage Books, 1962) and Morton White, *Science and Sentiment in America: Philosophical Thought from Jonathan Edwards to John Dewey* (New York: Oxford University Press, 1972).

[5] Bushnell, *God in Christ*, 92.

By "true theology" Bushnell had in mind something quite specific: "the exposition of Christian consciousness, as containing the divine."[6] In offering this definition, which made religious consciousness the primary datum for theological reflection, he negotiated the same corner that Schleiermacher had several decades earlier, and he explicitly proclaimed his solidarity with the newer current of German opinion represented by Richard Rothe.[7]

According to this conception of theology, claims about the authority of the Bible were to be rooted in and verified by the religious life. The authenticity of biblical revelation was not to be, could not be, speculatively demonstrated. Bushnell therefore dismisses both apologetical appeals to external evidences and dogmatic assertions of plenary verbal infallibility. The former, he contends, will at best satisfy the mind and leave the heart untouched; the latter will satisfy neither the mind nor the heart. Those who base biblical authority on an allegedly "punctually infallible and verbal inspiration" have chosen to rest their case on the least important and most vulnerable point. The discovery of even a single defect in the biblical records disproves their claims, and in light of textual criticism and the history of the canon, "the argument so stated must inevitably be lost; as, in fact, it always is."[8] It is, moreover, a superfluous argument, for even if the Bible were infallible, sinful humans could never attain "the sense of it as infallible . . . in any such manner of strictness and exact perception."[9] At any rate, the general principle that forecloses all such argumentation is this: intellectual assent to a concept of biblical authority is not the precondition, but the result, of religious awareness.

It is certainly true that *Nature and the Supernatural* contains an apologetic argument for the authenticity of biblical revelation: "All the capital points or ideas of Christianity, frame into the supernatural, on the one hand, in such a beautiful order and facility, and without any strain or contrivance or logical adaptation; and into human experience, on the other, in a way so consonant to the dignity of reason, and the wants and disabilities of sin, that the signature of God is plainly legible in the documents."[10] This argument, however, is altogether "internal," that is, it turns on the power of Christianity to evidence itself by addressing and transforming the human

6 Bushnell, *Christ in Theology*, 83–84.

7 Schleiermacher, *The Christian Faith*, §15: "Christian doctrines are accounts of the Christian religious affections set forth in speech." Bushnell (*Christ in Theology*, 84–85) claimed that "the ablest exposition" of the difference between theology and philosophy is that given by Richard Rothe. His allusion is to the translation of the Introduction to Rothe's *Theologische Ethik* given in J. D. Morrell's *Philosophy of Religion* (New York: D. Appleton, 1849). See Crosby, *Bushnell's Theory of Language*, 43–44.

8 Bushnell, *Nature and the Supernatural*, 33.

9 Ibid., 34.

10 Ibid., 34–35.

condition. Wary lest all "truth," even religious truth, be bound over to the method of science, "as if nothing could be true, save as it is proved by the scientific method," Bushnell calls for "a verification by the heart, and not by the notions of the head."[11]

This kind of reasoning is designed to admit, and to withstand, irrepressible doubts about many portions of the Bible. The premise is that "we establish God's infallibility only by a constructive use of generals, the particulars of which are conceived by us only in the faintest, most partial manner."[12] Thus Christianity will be intellectually vindicated when one realizes that its "prominent ideas, tokens, facts, and doctrines," which combine to form a scheme for "a spiritual renovation of souls," cannot be plausibly attributed to merely human action.[13] Yet in the final analysis this line of defense too must cross over from the realm of theory to that of personal conviction. Even after Bushnell has "demonstrated" that the message of salvation by faith is above but not contrary to reason, he must remind readers that its "truth" is confirmed only "in and by the immediate experience of the mind."[14]

As befits an apologist, the reminder was gently phrased in *Nature and the Supernatural*. The point had already been made with polemic force in *Christ in Theology*: religious experience alone verifies that the Bible is divinely revealed. The symbols of God in nature, history, and scripture present the "body" or "face" of divinity. But one learns, and so knows, that this is the case only when one experiences "the state of real divinity," "a living consciousness of God," which is ". . . derived to us from this and made conscious with us, by an immediate experience of God, in connection with this."[15] It is because the biblical symbols, together with the inner witness of the spirit, are constitutive of Christian consciousness that they may be said to be revelatory of God. The authenticity of biblical revelation is not a general truth of reason but a theological assertion, that is, an exposition of Christian consciousness.

So, too, is the assertion that the Bible is authoritative for theology. The circularity of this argument is premeditated. The "state of real divinity" is the basis for every theological claim, including that of biblical authority, and yet that state itself is derived from and bound to the biblical rhetoric of revelation. "Christian theology, then, is grounded in divinity, according to the old maxim, *Fides precedit intellectum*. Then, again, it rests on the Scripture body of fact, because in that, the divine is bodied and expressed, and offered to experience."[16] At issue here is a

---

[11] Ibid., 20.
[12] Ibid., 377.
[13] Ibid., 400, 376–79.
[14] Ibid., 379–80; see also 442, 520–28.
[15] Bushnell, *Christ in Theology*, 82–83.
[16] Ibid., 84.

realignment of relations among biblical text, theological judgment, and experiential piety. Whereas rational supernaturalism calls first for a theological judgment about biblical authority and then, second, for a life of faith congruent with that judgment, Bushnell calls first for a life of faith and then, second, for a theological judgment about biblical authority congruent with that life.

Implicit in this account is a quite specific construal of what it is about the Bible that is authoritative for theology. The references to "biblical fact" are not meant to call attention to historical facticity or to conceptual data.[17] They refer instead to the "fact-forms" or symbols in the Bible, and it is the patterning of these symbols that is crucial for Christian consciousness and Christian theology. Bushnell holds that as diverse as the symbols are they constitute a unity, and in two related senses. First, the two Testaments make up a typological whole, for the Hebrew religion provided the set of types that were later used in a second, spiritualized sense to set forth the gospel of the New Testament.[18] And, second, viewed as a whole the succession of biblical symbols makes up a cumulative portrait of the character of God. The pattern has at its center the figure of Jesus Christ, whom Bushnell considers the "form" of God. Thus he would have it that the truth of the Bible is confirmed when Jesus Christ, the form of God, becomes the form of the individual soul.[19]

What use is to be made of this symbolic pattern in the formulation of theological assertions? Bushnell's answer is clear: theology will be based on the Bible inasmuch as it seizes upon the symbols in order to express the contents of Christian consciousness. This is a work of the active imagination, which is to proceed from experience to symbol and into thought. The movement itself, Bushnell implies, is inevitable, for the

---

[17] Bushnell's theory of revelatory symbolism serves as what David Kelsey calls a "discrimen," i.e., a particular view of the mode of God's presence, which governs his conception of the authority and use of the Bible. Bushnell vacillates, however, in his construal of that discrimen, sometimes leaning toward a mode of objective actuality, which finds the meaning of the Bible in its symbolic description of the identity of God, and sometimes leaning toward the mode of ideal possibility, which relates the meaning of the texts to the transition from sin to grace. He clearly opposes, however, every attempt to construe the mode of God's presence in an ideational or conceptual mode, and he thereby repudiates the notion that biblical symbols can be translated into nonsymbolic concepts (see Kelsey, *The Uses of Scripture in Recent Theology* [Philadelphia: Fortress, 1975] 167–70).

[18] David Smith (*Symbolism and Growth*, 6–17) is perhaps to be credited as the first to draw proper attention to Bushnell's connection with the long evangelical tradition of typological interpretation—a viewpoint worthy of further study in light of recent scholarship on typology by Sacvan Bercovitch, *The Puritan Origins of the American Self* (New Haven: Yale University Press, 1975); idem, ed. *Typology and Early American Literature* (Amherst: University of Massachusetts Press, 1972); and Ursula Brumm, *American Thought and Religious Typology* (New Brunswick, NJ: Rutgers University Press, 1970).

[19] Bushnell, "Christ the Form of the Soul," *Spirit in Man*, 49.

inherent communicativeness of the social self insures that Christian consciousness, like all consciousness, will be "exposited." In this sense theology arises quite naturally out of religion. A passage in *Forgiveness and Law* explains what happens: "In the original word of Scripture the truths revealed are either visibly or verbally presented. . . . Being given to intelligence, intelligence will fall at work upon them, and the human thought laboring in the outward images of things, will generate modes of speech and laws of experience that compose a kind of second language on the base-level of nature."[20] The result is a distinctive form of discourse that is a tensive admixture of image and concept, namely, doctrinal theology.

Such a theology, Bushnell insists, can never present a precise, exhaustive, definitive account of the essence of Christianity. The Bible offers no such theoretical system and language can bear no such burden. For three reasons, in particular, is the theologian to be humble. First, theological expressivity can never attain literal exactitude: "The truth-feeling power of the soul may have truth present immediately to it, or may directly intuit truth, without symbols or representations of language. But the moment it will think discursively, or represent to another any subject of thought, that thought must be clothed in forms that are only signs or analogies, and not equivalent of truth."[21] Second, even a theology that seeks to express "a real state of divinity" will be tainted by much that is not divine, "just according to the degree of human defect or mistake there is in it, which is probably a large subtraction."[22] Third, the language of theology will be organically related, and therefore relative, to the personal and cultural setting within which it emerges. At best, then, theological statements set forth "the seeing of the authors, at the precise stand-point occupied by them, at the time, and they are true only as seen from that point,—not even there, save in a proximate sense."[23]

Forgetful of these limits, theologians have imposed their speculative constructions on those who seek faith, participate in the church, and read the Bible, and it is this imposition that Bushnell cannot abide. Creeds, catechisms, and systems, he maintains, may be valued as expressions but not as tests of religion. Their contents should be reinvestigated "every fifty years," and their formulations should be "held in a spirit of accommodation, not as laws of belief but as bodies of sound sense and understanding."[24] Were it not so crucial, it could perhaps go without

---

[20] Horace Bushnell, *Forgiveness and Law, Grounded in Principles Interpreted by Human Analogies* (2d ed.; New York: Scribner, Armstrong; London: Hodder and Stoughton, 1875) 15–16; in 1877 republished as vol. 2 of *The Vicarious Sacrifice* (New York: Charles Scribner). All citations herein refer to the pagination of the 1877 edition.

[21] Bushnell, *Christ in Theology*, 15.

[22] Ibid., 84.

[23] Ibid., 80.

[24] Bushnell, *God in Christ*, 81.

saying that one of the by-products of such doctrinal latitudinarianism—often associated with nineteenth-century liberalism—is a new freedom for the biblical scholar. Despite his reluctance to foster a thoroughgoing "historical-critical" scholarship of the Bible, Bushnell contributed to its rise by removing some of the obstacles that New England theology put in its path.[25]

At the same time Bushnell had drawn attention to the historicality of theology. His response to that discomforting thought was to point to its potential benefits. Theology might succeed by capitalizing on its weaknesses. That it is symbolic, impure, and historically relative meant that it could reengage the biblical symbols time and again and draw forth their meaning in each age. The very effort to do so would, he thought, be of practical value to the church. It would attest that Christians are committed to the God whose truth encompasses the knowledge that comes from both faith and science. It would confirm that Christianity is not a religion that "begins and ends in unintelligible vagaries." And it would restrain those "visionary flights, erratic fancies and wild hallucinations" that might otherwise pass for piety. Here, then, anti-intellectualism, too, reached its limit. Those who rely on the reason alone to supply their religion, Bushnell claims, end up skeptics or rationalists. Those who rely only on the emotions abandon Christianity in favor of mysticism. What is needed is a theology in which the head and the heart "walk together, never so truly agreed as when they agree to hold each other."[26]

Above all, Bushnell granted theology the same value as any other act of communication. An exposition of Christian consciousness is a means by which one person shares an experience with another. The moral tendency argument, which judged the adequacy of theological statements in terms of their ability to elicit moral and religious growth, had already become standard fare in the New England tradition.[27] Given Bushnell's view of communication, it becomes the operative norm for judging the validity of any theology. The doctrine of the Trinity, for example, can be defended as a "practical truth" that expands Christian consciousness.

---

[25] John Dillenberger and Claude Welch, *Protestant Christianity, Interpreted through its Development* (New York: Charles Scribner's Sons, 1954) 197; see also the Epilogue below.

[26] Bushnell, *God in Christ*, 310–17, esp. 316.

[27] Citing the anonymous author of *A Review of the Rev. Dr. Channing's discourse, preached at the dedication of the Second Congregational Unitarian Church, New York, December 7, 1826* (Boston, 1827), pp. 3–13, C. H. Faust notes that the conflict betwen Unitarianism and orthodoxy had moved through two phases and had entered a third. The first used biblical literature as the main appeal in argument; the second, philosophy; and the third, moral tendency—"the 'main question' being 'which of the two systems, the Unitarian or the Orthodox, is of superior tendency to form an elevated religious character'" ("The Background of the Unitarian Opposition to Transcendentalism," *Modern Philology* 35 [1938] 297–98). See also Brown, *Biblical Criticism in America*, 60–74.

> We do not mean, it is hardly necessary to say, that the Trinity is practical in the sense of presenting some thing to be done or practiced. Neither is it practical in the sense of showing in what manner something else is to be done. It is practical only as an instrument of thought, action, self-application to all the great matters of faith. . . . By the Christian Trinity it is that our sense of God is opened; what he has done for us and will do, put in terms of use. . . .[28]

All theology is to be a practical truth in just this sense. "It is even useful or necessary," Bushnell asserts, "as a re-acting basis for the mind, in climbing into a divine experience."[29]

This marriage of the heart and the head requires that the theologian stay as close as possible to the biblical symbols, resisting the temptation to fix on the forms at the expense of their full orbit of meaning. "Having gotten the truth," Bushnell explains, "we want modesty enough not to take our spiritual discernings into our natural judgment, to be shaped and manipulated there—modesty enough not to assume that we can go beyond the scriptures and body into science and fixed articles of divinity, what they, for want of sufficient medium, never attempted."[30] But this technique is commended by more than modesty alone. Only by this means can one trade on the expressive power of the texts and propagate the forms that have already demonstrated their power to transform human life. The secret of a successful theology will be its ability to prolong the meaning of biblical symbols, to explore their implications within changing intellectual settings, and to intensify their impact upon life in the present. The aesthetic force of biblical terms is to be preserved, and this is possible only if the terms are cultivated, not discarded.

Cultivation obviously depended upon a biblical study sensitive to poetic forms of life, even though theology was not itself a poem. But it also depended on a biblical study sensitive to the dangers that came with any attempt to deal with antiquated language. Bushnell expected the theologian to "justify the language of scripture, and be clear of any real absurdity," and to "get the declarative work of the Bible grafted in upon the natural analogies, where it will be so much closer to the common life of men, and settle its hold just so much more firmly on the convictions."[31] These mandates make it plain that Bushnell was willing to face up to the historicality of the interpreter's own frame of reference. But they also make it evident that this willingness would come into conflict with his desire to stay with and in the biblical symbols.

---

[28] Bushnell, "The Christian Trinity A Practical Truth," *Building Eras in Religion*, 110.
[29] Bushnell, *Christ in Theology*, 87.
[30] Bushnell, *God in Christ*, 308–9.
[31] Ibid., 136, 160; idem, *Forgiveness and Law, Grounded in Principles Interpreted by Human Analogies* (New York: Scribner, Armstrong, 1874) 16.

The "justification" of biblical language was a goal shared by many evangelicals committed to modern standards of meaningfulness and validity. It was, after all, one thing to praise the "foolishness" of the gospel and quite another to concede its "real absurdity." An interest in interpreting the Bible by reference to natural analogies was a bit more unusual. That preachers would search for familiar yet poignant illustrations from everyday experience in order to drive home the meaning of a biblical text was to be expected. That the procedure would be an indispensable part of theological method was a novel suggestion indeed.

The problem that gave rise to this proposal was itself neither new nor insignificant. Unless biblical, and theological, language makes contact with lived experience it remains dark and unassimilable. "The sin of all our theologic endeavor in the past ages," he claims, is that theologians use terms that have "no reality and no assignable meaning."[32] His complaint has by now become a commonplace. But his strategy for resolving the problem illustrates that his brand of liberalism would place restrictions of its own on the biblical interpreter. At the very outset it must be assumed "that nothing can be true of God, or of Christ, which is not true in some sense *more humano*, and is not made intelligible by human analogies. We can not interpret God . . . except by what we find in our own personal instincts and ideas."[33] Here the analogical connection between signifier and signified is made subject to an *analogia entis* between the infinite and the finite.

It must be admitted that this interpretive principle does not appear until Bushnell's last published book. Its appearance there, however, only makes explicit what had been hitherto unstated. He studied the biblical symbols in order to make new discoveries, but at the end of the study he frequently discovered what was already suspected, if not already known, by Christians steeped in Yankee culture. His proposals for the treatment of the Bible were intended to free the biblical texts from the strictures of culture-bound assumptions and to allow them to lay their claims, however discomforting or surprising, upon contemporary life. But in reading the Bible he found it hard to resist the claims that contemporary life laid upon the texts. The conflict was built into his work, and it reappears again and again in his own constructive theology.

[32] Bushnell, *Forgiveness and Law*, 13.
[33] Ibid., 12–13.

VI

SENSIBILITY TO SIN

"As beings of intelligence we find ourselves hedged in by mystery on every side."[1] With these words Bushnell invited his parishioners to ponder their human condition. And by seizing upon an image offered in the book of Job (37:12), "and now men see not the bright light which is in the clouds," he contrasted the imperfection of life as it is, a life under a cloud, with the perfection of life as it should be, irradiated by divine light. In this sermon, "Light on the Cloud," the discrepancy between what is and what should be is traced to the core of human selfhood, where it appears first and foremost as an all-too-human dilemma: the self, a self-conscious being, is "a deep and inscrutable mystery" even to itself.[2]

Since Bushnell held that religion is life, he regarded the human dilemma as at root a religious dilemma and, as such, effectively addressed only by religious resources. In his day this opinion had not yet become eccentric, but it was certainly contestable. Thus, the sermon "Self-Examination Examined" broached a matter of controversy. Contained in it was a warning against all those who advised insecure folk to seek self-knowledge and, by implication, self-mastery on their own. This, Bushnell asserted, was a counsel of despair. The attempt to know oneself "by a direct act of voluntary self-inspection, must be fruitless," and in any case the only sort of examination that counts is that "accomplished under and through the scrutiny, or inspecting power of God; we truly prove ourselves, when he proves us, and may rightly approve ourselves, only when he approves us."[3] This is hardly an unexpected word, coming as it does from an evangelical preacher. What is of interest, however, is the particular way Bushnell handled biblical symbols in order to administer the examination.

One biblical symbol above all, he believed, illumined the mystery of the human condition and identified the discrepancy between existence as

---

[1] Bushnell, "Light on the Cloud," *Sermons for the New Life* (New York: Charles Scribner, 1858) 144.

[2] Ibid., 151.

[3] Bushnell, "Self-examination Examined," *Sermons on Living Subjects*, 230, 227.

it is and existence as it should be. As he put it in *Nature and the Supernatural*, "the groaning and travailing in pain together of the whole creation—it is all the supernatural work, the bad miracle of sin. No other name will fitly name it."[4] The mere availability of the word, however, did not insure its proper use and understanding. That human life was less than perfect, few even in optimistic mid-century New England would care to deny, and in the backwash of Puritanism there remained something of a cultural consensus that the word sin should figure in any assessment of the human condition. But how it should be figured in was by no means obvious. "Simple as the word is," Bushnell observed, "and on the lips of every body (as we know it to be), there is yet no virtual agreement connected with the word."[5] Subjected to such varying interpretations, its significatory power had dissipated.

The conflict of interpretation that Bushnell had noted was due in large part to the fact that the meaning of the word depended on the frame of reference within which it was set. In the theological anthropology of Puritanism, it had been laced together with other terms—the fall, depravity, divine decrees, imputation, and the like—descriptive of the plight of the soul alienated from the affections of the sovereign God. Forceful advocates of this tradition, the like of John Cotton or Jonathan Edwards, might couple this bleak picture of human nature with affirmations of God's excellence and of the delights of the regenerate soul. But with each passing decade of the eighteenth and the nineteenth century the coupling came under increasing stress.

Viewed as the whole, the history of New England theology shows that even the pious faced mounting difficulties in trying to speak of sin as more than particular, deliberate violations of religious and moral precepts. In the context of enlightened notions of benevolence, justice, and culpability, traditional language about original sin especially became problematic. Modern sensibilities, it would seem, were inclined toward a morally perfect God, a morally accountable humanity, and a morally estimable relationship between the two. And this inclination, of course, was a key stimulus for the "changing conceptions of original sin" that arose in the course of orthodox disputes with Arminians, Unitarians, and free thinkers of every sort. Strict Calvinists were placed on the defensive, and repeated efforts were made—one thinks of Samuel Hopkins and Nathaniel W. Taylor especially—to salvage the tradition by modifying it.[6]

---

4 Bushnell, *Nature and the Supernatural*, 218.

5 Bushnell, *God in Christ*, 47.

6 H. Shelton Smith, *Changing Conceptions of Original Sin: A Study in American Theology since 1750* (New York: Charles Scribner's Sons, 1958) chaps. 4–7. Edward Clinton Gardiner has written two fine articles on Bushnell's views: "Horace Bushnell's Concept of Responses: A Fresh Approach to the Doctrine of Ability and Inability," *Religion in Life* 27 (1957–58) 119–31; "Horace Bushnell's Doctrine of Depravity," *Theology Today* 12 (1955) 10–26.

Bushnell had doubts of his own about the tradition. He came to agree with Taylor that "the sin of no person can be transmitted, as a sin, or charged to the account of another," and he assured his Unitarian friend Cyrus Bartol that "the old notion of a total depravity, and of being damned for what God made us to be," was justly dismissed as "folly."[7] Indeed, he went so far as to admit that "there is a susceptibility to good, in every mind. . . . The soul has that within it, which may be appealed to by what is right and holy."[8] Yet beyond this he would not go. Even though he joined the Unitarians in rejecting orthodox theories of sin, he could not share their optimism about the human condition.

He arrived at this position relatively early in his career. In *Views of Christian Nurture* he wrote: "Under the old categories of original sin, federal headship and the like, cast away by many, ridiculed by not a few, there lies a great and momentous truth, announced by reason as well as by scripture—that in Adam all men died and that by one man's disobedience they were made sinners, that death had passed upon men for that all have sinned."[9] This view he held throughout his life. As he told Bartol, the "Christian difference" that separated them had to do with the connection between sin and a fall.[10]

In mid-career Bushnell turned to combat yet another, and in his judgment even more dangerous, interpretation of sin. Modern exponents of naturalism, he charged, explained the term by reference to "mere cause and effect in nature."[11] Several names were mentioned in his indictment. Parker was cited for reducing the "bitter wrongs" of humanity to "developments of 'discordant causes'" in an otherwise sound nature; Fourier, for claiming "that what we call sin, by a kind of misnomer, is predicable only of society, not of the individual man"; and Strauss, for holding that sin is only "the personal mischief or defect" which individuals exhibit "in the 'blameless' course of human progress." And popular literature of the sort produced by Carlyle and Emerson was judged to "exalt and glorify it [sin], by placing both it and virtue upon the common footing of a natural use and necessity."[12]

According to Bushnell, such naturalistic accounts all come to focus on a common meaning for the word sin—misdirection. "This word *misdirection* has the advantage that it slips all recognition of blame or responsibility because it brings into view no real agency or responsible

---

[7] Bushnell, *Views of Christian Nurture*, 1st ed., p. 192; Cheyney, *Life and Letters*, 229.

[8] Bushnell, *Views of Christian Nurture, and of Subjects Adjacent Thereto* (2d ed.; Hartford: E. Hunt, 1848) 90.

[9] *Views of Christian Nurture*, 1st ed., 192.

[10] Cheyney, *Life and Letters*, 227.

[11] Bushnell, *Nature and the Supernatural*, 145.

[12] Ibid., 145–48.

agent. And hence it becomes a favorite word, and is formally proposed by many advocates of naturalism, as the philosophic synonym of sin."[13] This definition, however, leaves open the very issue that the word sin is to address: how is the mysterious source of misdirection to be characterized?

In exploring the significatory power of sin, then, Bushnell contended with orthodox theories to his right and with Unitarian and naturalistic views to his left. The solution could not be to run up the middle, for in his judgment both sides were to be faulted for making so little of the word:

> It is either nothing, or else it is a great deal more than it is conceived to be by the multitude who admit its existence. The mental and moral philosophers make nothing of it, going on to construct their sciences, so called, precisely as if the soul had received no shock of detriment; and even the most orthodox theologians do scarcely more than score it with guilty conviction, regarding it seldom as a dynamic force, and then with a comprehension too restricted to allow any true impression, of its import.[14]

The impression he had of its import may be gathered from his treatment of several biblical passages.

The Genesis account of Adam—the innocent, the disobedient, the accursed—was obviously near the top of Bushnell's list of biblical materials most in need of reinterpretation. Like so many others of the day, Bushnell believed that orthodox theories of original sin had so emphasized the inevitability of the fall and the consequent total depravity of human nature that the very principle of moral accountability had been undermined. Yet he was also convinced that those who denied that sin involved a fall of humanity failed to acknowledge how limited was the human capacity for attaining the good life apart from divine assistance. In his judgment, right-wing views were over-determinations of the biblical symbols in the name of dogmatism; left-wing views, under-determinations in the name of optimism.

Nature and the Supernatural deals at considerable length with the concept of sin. The goal is to offer a rationally persuasive statement of its nature and effects. The arguments are many and complex, and it will suffice to lift up a few main points relating to the interpretation of the story of Adam. According to Bushnell, reason attests that a divine plan which includes the creation and perfection of free agents must allow for the "caprices of liberty."[15] It is just this that he finds narrated in the Bible. Freshly created, Adam is an innocent who faces the future with

---

[13] Ibid., 163.
[14] Ibid., 217–18.
[15] Ibid., 99.

freedom. But freedom is indeterminacy, and in his first choice for good or for evil Adam will shape his character. God has not foreordained the selection; natural necessity has not governed it. That Adam chooses to transgress God's law is therefore an incalculable act of freedom.[16]

This account of innocence is obviously intended to dispel the cloud of doom that the orthodox often associated with Adam's life in paradise. It is counterbalanced, however, by an analysis of the perils of innocence that would sober those who long for the joys of primal existence. The innocence of indeterminacy is said to be "a moral state that is only inchoate, or incomplete, lacking something not yet reached, which is necessary to the probable rejection of evil."[17] It is a human nature endowed with the "necessary ideas" of the true, the right, the good. But it is also a state of jeopardy, a "condition privative," which lacks "the empirical knowledge of what these mean in actual experience," and "a course of government" that implants the law of duty firmly within the self, and the strength to fend off evil influences.[18] Bushnell therefore concludes:

> These conditions privative are in the nature of perils, and while they excuse nothing, for the law of duty is always plain, they are yet drawn so close to the soul and open their gulfs, on either hand, so deep, that our expectation of the fall is really as pressing as if it were determined by some law that annihilates liberty. Liberty we know is not annihilated. And yet we say, looking on the state of man made perilous, in this manner, by liberty, that we can not expect him to stand.[19]

The fall is certain, but, as R. W. B. Lewis puts it, "fortunate."[20] Beyond the innocence of indeterminacy is perfection—the telos of human nature. And perfection is attained only by an encounter with evil and a victory over it. It is this that God plans for in permitting the fall and preparing a deliverance for fallen creatures.

This interpretation of Adam's fall turns on the conception of sin most widely accepted in popular opinion—that of a "blameable action," "a transgression of right," or "a disobedience of God."[21] Bushnell emphasizes throughout that the figure of Adam represents an original condition of humanity and need not be taken as a historical individual. In *The Vicarious Sacrifice*, these same premises result in a concise statement of the "meaning" of Genesis 3.

Noting that many scholars, "even those who do not favor 'mythical interpretations,'" will grant that the primeval history is "in some proper

16 Ibid., 128.
17 Ibid., 108.
18 Ibid., 108–28.
19 Ibid., 128.
20 Lewis, *American Adam*, 66–73.
21 Bushnell, *Nature and the Supernatural*, 141.

sense, a myth," Bushnell too is willing to allow the point. Like any form of literature, he says, myth may communicate truth, "and it may be that a myth occurs in revelation, just because there is, at the time, no culture of thought, and philosophy, and reflective reason, deep enough to express, or conceive the matter given, in a way of didactic statement."[22] In this case, however, the ascent into the meaning of the myth leads to the realm of allegory:

> The eternal law of right is a tree, and the knowledge of good and evil a fruit that hangs on it, and the declared threatenings of death, notifications of the consequences otherwise unknown. Temptation figures in the story as a serpent, and the new-begun race are summoned to a conflict with him, and an assured triumph over him. Then pass out the sad pair, excluded from all possible self-recovery, as if fenced away by the flashing swords of cherubim, to work and suffer, and conquer, as God and his Son will help them.[23]

Sin as transgression is a rejection of the "Law of Right," which is both the essence of divine perfection and the image of God inherent in the human soul as its "Monarch Principle."[24]

According to Bushnell, the "fitness" of linking "the first sin" and the "original law of duty" in this way is "because that law is really pronounced in the simple fact of being a moral nature."[25] The details of the account, for example, whether the act of transgression was "touching a tree, or tasting a fruit," play no role in the determination of the essential meaning of the story. And that essential meaning can be stated quite plainly in terms other than the symbols themselves: "everlasting right is cast away, and the golden harmony of right dissolved."[26]

How does Adam's original sin—whether it be history or myth—relate to the human condition? In *Nature and the Supernatural* the answer comes by the reference to what reason would likely infer to be the results of primal transgression and what experience confirms to be the case. The picture that Bushnell paints is dark. The violation of law disturbs "the crystalline order" of the faculties of selfhood, and, because of the connection of mind and body, the health of the entire organism is impaired. Once introduced, this "great disordering principle" disrupts the intersubjective bond that links each individual to every other and turns the order of nature into "a realm of deformity and aberration."[27] The ultimate result is that the

---

[22] Horace Bushnell, *The Vicarious Sacrifice, Grounded in Principles Interpreted by Human Analogies* (New York: Charles Scribner's Sons, 1877) 1:249.

[23] Ibid.

[24] Ibid., 250.

[25] Ibid.

[26] Ibid.

[27] Bushnell, *Nature and the Supernatural*, chap. 6. In chap. 7 Bushnell accounts for much of the disorder within the natural order itself as an "anticipative consequence" of the fall.

world and everyone in it become accursed.

It will not matter, then, whether one believes that the human race descended from Adam and Eve or whether one believes, "as is now strenuously asserted by some, both on grounds of science and of scripture interpretation," that there was more than a single pair of human parents. In either case, "the genus humanity is still a single genus comprehending the races"; they had their origin at some time; they sinned.[28] Given this fact, "the principles of physiology" dictate that the progeny of beings impaired by sin will be "constituently injured or depravated." Although their actions may be "innocent," they will be born in an unhealthy state, which "the scriptures, in a certain popular, comprehensive way, sometimes call 'sin'; because it is a condition of depravation that may well enough be taken as the root of a guilty, sinning life."[29] The Bible makes no attempt "to settle metaphysically the point where personal guilt commences," but its description of the curse placed upon the universe tells of a truth that cannot be denied. "Call it then a myth, disallow the notion of a positive infliction as being unphilosophical; still the matter of the change, or general world-lapse asserted in it, is one of the grandest, most massive, best-attested truths included in human knowledge."[30]

This strategy for connecting sin and the fall with the imperfection of existence rescues the biblical symbols from the literalism of orthodoxies and from the neglect of modernizers. The achievement, however, takes its toll on Bushnell's hermeneutical integrity. In order to vindicate the truth of the symbols, their significatory power is depleted by rational analysis, allegory, and paraphrase. That is, despite his intentions Bushnell ends up with names other than "sin" that fitly name the groaning and travailing of creation—transgression of law, disorder, and the laws of physiology.

But there are other occasions when Bushnell allows the "liveliness" or metaphoric reach of biblical symbols to come into play more strongly. Foremost among them are those that explore the meaning of sin by reference to an "interpersonal" relationship between God and humanity. The parable of the Prodigal Son in Luke, for example, leads him to suggest that the "hunger of the soul" is the hunger of sin—a torment caused because the soul is "separated from God and the true bread of life in him."[31] And in interpreting Paul's reference to those who lack "the knowledge of God" (1 Cor 15:34), he applies the text to all those who, like the Corinthians, know about God "in the traditional and merely cognitive way," but who are shut off by sin from an immediate awareness of the divine presence.[32]

28 Ibid., 177.
29 Ibid., 177–78.
30 Ibid., 194.
31 Bushnell, "The Hunger of the Soul," *Sermons for the New Life*, 78–79.
32 Bushnell, "The Immediate Knowledge of God," *Sermons on Living Subjects*, 114–28.

It is on such occasions that he most often voices concerns that go against the grain of the moralism so common in his own works and in those of his contemporaries. In the sermon "Respectable Sin" he warns that even "what is generally called virtue, and passes for a virtuous character," may still be sin. "The evil spirit called sin may be trained up to politeness, and made to be genteel sin; it may be elegant, cultivated sin; it may be industrious, thrifty sin; it may be a great political manager, a great commercial operator, a great inventor; it may be learned, scientific, eloquent, highly poetic sin; still it is sin."[33] What is identified as the problem with virtue in this sermon is the same as that which Bushnell describes as the problem with religious sentiment, good works, philanthropy, self-culture, and social reform in other sermons—it is "the state of being without God, or out of allegiance with God."[34] Here the word sin cannot be replaced by the word transgression, for it is a transgression that is also an alienation. The multivalence of the word makes its use indispensable and inexhaustible.

Bushnell also speaks of a biblical symbolism that is unique in its power to bring about a true sensibility—that is, not just an idea, but an experience—of the human condition under sin. "There is sensibility enough to wrongs suffered," he explains in *Forgiveness and Law*, "and a considerable sense of wrongs done. But these are sins only, not sin."[35] In the story of Jesus Christ, however, and especially in the passion narrative, "there is to be a new sensibility to sin, not only in individual persons, but in the world itself, such as never before was observed."[36] Because the passion *narrates* the tragedy of God incarnate, it discloses as no abstract statement can that sin is a personal rejection of God.

The "truth" of the story is communicated, Bushnell contends, through the dramatic presentation of the character of Christ:

> If he [Christ] is a fiction only, or a myth, a romance gotten up by three or four of the most unromantic writers of the world, still he is the greatest, solidest, most real, truth ever known to man. The mere conception of such a life and character is inherently eternal. . . . It affirms itself eternally as light, by its own self-evidence, and the soul of guilt trembles inwardly before it.[37]

Those who come to know this character through the gospel story are to be

---

[33] Bushnell, "Respectable Sin," *Sermons for the New Life*, 332–33.

[34] Ibid., 333. See also, e.g., idem, "Christian Forgiveness" and "The Putting on of Christ," *Christ and His Salvation: In Sermons Variously Related Thereto* (New York: Charles Scribner, 1864) 385, 431–32; idem, *Nature and the Supernatural*, 512–14; idem, "Religious Nature, and Religious Character," *Sermons on Living Subjects*, 130–32, 139; idem, "The Spirit in Man" and "Christ as Separate from the World," *Sermons for the New Life* 29, 34, 451–52, 455; idem, "Sin in Noble Things," *Spirit in Man*, 251.

[35] Bushnell, *Forgiveness and Law*, 226.

[36] Ibid., 225

[37] Bushnell, "Conviction of Sin by the Cross," *Christ and His Salvation*, 132.

taken up by it: "So, when the Son of God is crucified and expelled to be seen no more, not the spectators only of the scene, but all we that pierced him by our sin were to be visited with guilty, soul-humbling pains in like manner."[38] Here the ascent into meaning leads to a new, and terrifying, experience.

According to Bushnell, the cross engages the imagination and the feeling and generates "a new conscience" with respect to relationship to God. "Jews and Pagans had before been made conscious at times of particular sin; we are made conscious, in a deeper and more appalling way, of the state of sin itself, the damning evil that infects our humanity at its root—that which rejected and crucified the Son of God, and is in fact, the general madness and lost condition of the race."[39] Whether the truth of the passion could survive a sentimental retelling of the story is a question much in doubt. But at least in this case Bushnell's interpretive practice is in keeping with his interpretation theory.

Adam and Christ, each in his own way a fallen innocent, and the multivalent word sin—these symbols, according to Bushnell, bring humanity to self-knowledge. Despite his penchant for didactic exposition, Bushnell could not dispense with the symbols. An examination of human nature may ascertain the conditions that make it possible for the self to renounce its primal freedom, and a sober assessment of the miseries of nature, history, and personal life might document the ruin of humanity. But the biblical symbols suggest what neither introspection nor analysis descry: misery is due to an act of transgression that is at the same time an act of betrayal.

[38] Ibid., 134.
[39] Ibid., 135–36.

VII
THE CHARACTER OF JESUS

Of all the symbols in the Bible, none was more important to Bushnell than the figure of Jesus Christ. "After all," he wrote in a personal letter, "there is not very much in the Bible, or anywhere else, besides Jesus Christ."[1] Others might have preferred to speak more guardedly, but there can be no doubt that the remark is indicative of the ever-increasing Christocentrism of nineteenth-century theology. It was not by accident, then, that Bushnell devoted so much of his biblical and theological study to Christological issues. In his preoccupation with Jesus, however, he did not by any means merely repeat well-worn evangelical clichés or merely tinker with well-established scholastic views. The kind of attention he gave to the person and work of Christ demonstrated that he was concerned about the very possibility of Christology.[2]

This question, like every other, was to be handled with due regard for the rhetoric of revelation. The centrality of Christ was consequently developed in terms highly unusual for the day. Just as God's revelation in nature, history, and scripture was said to be "metaphor upon metaphor," so the figure of Jesus was said to be "God's last metaphor," the master image around which every other revolved. And the deliverance from sin brought about through Jesus Christ was said to be an event depending upon the power of artistic expression. Thus, a Christology that set forth an exposition of Christian consciousness would gather up and elaborate "all the metaphoric meanings" of the life and death of Jesus.[3]

Even in the way he posed the issues, then, Bushnell called for an approach unlike that which he found among his contemporaries. A proper estimate of the figure of Jesus Christ was to be derived from a biblical study sensitive to poetic forms of life and a theological study distinguished by a nicer and more cultivated apprehension of symbols. His works contain numerous examples of the sort of studies he had in mind. Surveying the biblical references to the humanity and the divinity of Christ, for example, he proposed that the two-natures doctrine associated with the incarnation

---

[1] Cheyney, *Life and Letters*, 478.
[2] Welch, *Protestant Thought*, 141–46.
[3] Bushnell, "Our Gospel A Gift," *Building Eras in Religion*, 259.

be viewed as a way of speaking of the manifestation of God's power in history rather than as a theoretical solution to a scientific problem about the interiority of Jesus. Likewise, the doctrine of the Trinity was to be understood as a collocation of symbols—God as Father, as Son, and as Spirit—which by their illogical unity raise the mind to a truth about the divine nature without destroying its mystery.

Throughout these Christological reflections, the focus is placed on Jesus Christ as an expressive symbol, whose personal character communicated the character of God. For this reason it is altogether appropriate to look to Bushnell's presentation of the character of Jesus in order to illustrate the treatment accorded biblical materials. A section of *Nature and the Supernatural* is of particular interest, because it represents a miniature, and minor, contribution to the study of the historical Jesus.

Chapter X of *Nature and the Supernatural* was one of Bushnell's most resolute attempts to identify the significance of the figure Jesus Christ. Its title is a summary of the thesis: "The Character of Jesus Forbids His Possible Classification with Men." In its day it passed as something of an apologetical tour de force, selected for republication separately in book form.[4] It is a sentimentalized personality sketch of Jesus—more of a compilation than a reconstruction of the gospels. Yet this feature only heightens its historical significance, for it demonstrates that Bushnell was early on responsive to the growing public and scholarly interest in a nondogmatic portrait of Jesus. The central figure encountered in this simple and comprehensive reading of the gospels is a human Jesus who is more than human—a Jesus who is the symbolic manifestation of God, a God-man. But this is a God-man who is less remote, more benign, more humanly approachable than that depicted in orthodox theologies. And in focusing on the character of Jesus, Bushnell helped introduce evangelical Protestants to a quite modern strategy—a Christology *von unten nach oben*.[5]

The chapter was but one link in a chain of arguments designed to prove that Christianity offered a supernatural redemption. Previous chapters were to show that such a ministration was not only possible but necessary in light of the relationship between God and humanity. Since the "grand peculiarity" of the Bible was its claim that this ministration was established in Jesus Christ, the discussion of the character of Jesus was a decisive next step in the argument. Here one found "adequate evidence" for this crucial biblical claim: "On the single question, therefore, of the more than human character of Jesus, we propose, in perfect confidence, to rest a principal argument for Christianity as a supernatural institution; for,

---

[4] Horace Bushnell, *The Character of Jesus: Forbidding His Possible Classification with Men* (New York: Charles Scribner, 1861), which later appeared in Scottish, English, and Spanish editions.

[5] Welch, *Protestant Thought*, 266.

if there be in Jesus a character which is not human, then has something broken into the world that is not of it, and the spell of unbelief is broken."[6]

Apologetics demanded that Bushnell bracket any assumptions about the historicity of the gospels. It was, after all, just this point that the "critics in the school of naturalism" had called into question. Thus, whatever was to be said about the character and the historicity of Jesus must be based on an analysis of the gospel texts themselves. "We open the book," Bushnell explains, "and discover in it four distinct biographies of a certain remarkable character, called Jesus Christ." Admitting that modern readers might well find the gospel stories of this character "too extravagant for belief" and be tempted to put the book down, he nonetheless believes that their interest will be held by "the sense of something very peculiar in the character of this remarkable person."[7]

The bulk of the chapter is devoted to a retelling of words, deeds, incidents, and descriptions in the gospels, which go to form the literary portrait of Jesus. Drawn from these are the elements exhibiting the key features of his character—his perfect youth, his harmless yet sublime innocence, his sinlessness, his attitude and his behavior in dealing with others, and his response to his sufferings. The result is a gospel harmony—details selectively gathered into vignettes arranged in a loosely chronological, or narrative, order. The movement from scene to scene is to have the cumulative effect of introducing readers to a "man" who is "a holy thing."[8] As the story unfolds, it depicts a protagonist who is unique—not only in the sense that every literary figure differs from every other but also in the sense that this particular literary figure is a human being with personal characteristics superior to those of anyone else known in literature or history. Apart from dogmatic or historical considerations, this reading of the gospels as literature yields the identity of a distinctive individual: "Jesus, the Christ; manifestly not human, not of our world—some being who has burst into it, and is not of it."[9]

The question then becomes whether this person who exists in the texts is to be judged to have existed in history as well. The alternatives are "either that such a character actually lived, and was possible to be described, because it furnished the matter of the picture, itself; or else, that Jesus, being a merely human character as he lived, was adorned or set off in this manner, by the exaggerations of fancy, and fable, and wild tradition afterward."[10] Bushnell does not bother to ask if the character may be a product of artistic creativity pure and simple, but the factors

---

[6] Bushnell, *Nature and the Supernatural*, 278.

[7] Ibid., 277.

[8] Ibid., 322.

[9] Ibid.

[10] Ibid., 323.

he brings to bear on the second alternative would apply to this possibility as well. In either case the picture of the God-man would have to be explained by reference to human abilities—religious and literary.

The first alternative, Bushnell notes, strains human credibility: "we can believe any miracle . . . more easily than that Christ was a man, and yet a perfect character, such as here is given."[11] Yet the second alternative is even less likely. One would have to assume that four gospel writers, who were "widely distinguished in their style and mental habit—inferior persons, all, as regards their accomplishments, and none of them remarkable for their gifts of genius," and "children all of credulity, retailing the absurd gossip and the fabulous stories of an age of marvels," were nonetheless able to produce works that combine to present "the only perfect character known to mankind."[12] And since this assumption could be held only in "a more credulous age" than that of the evangelists themselves, Bushnell concludes that the rational course is to affirm the historicity of the gospel account.[13]

This is not an easy argument to classify. It is certainly more literary than dogmatic or historical. Yet in treating the gospels as literature Bushnell will at times heed and at times overlook significant details. In the final analysis one must say that it is primarily psychological, and in two respects. First, as gospel interpretation it subordinates everything to a single psychological category—character. In this it finds whatever unity there is to the story, and by this it judges what is and is not salient to the plot. The resurrection, for example, is never mentioned. From the standpoint of historical study, one might debate whether the resurrection is an event to be included in an account of the *historical* Jesus. In a literary study, however, its omission is telling.

One must suspect that Bushnell does not find the resurrection either determinative or illustrative of the character of Jesus, even as a literary figure. And the suspicion is confirmed when one observes that the character which is sketched is one of pure inwardness. It is a psychic constitution that displays itself in external relations but is never shaped by them. Literary incident, then, contributes to the depiction of the character of Jesus only insofar as it is the occasion for an outward exhibition of inner life. The resurrection does not fit into this scheme, because it is neither an expression of nor an occasion for the expression of the inner self of Jesus. It is an event that intrudes into what Bushnell has identified as the story line and therefore is excluded from his account altogether.

Second, the move from the literary to the historical Jesus goes beyond literary-historical judgment to rest on a (pre-)conception about

11 Ibid.
12 Ibid., 323–24.
13 Ibid., 324.

psychological perfection. This was in actuality a deft reworking of otherwise familiar arguments. It was by no means unusual for one to claim that the correspondence between the ideal humanity portrayed in Jesus and that projected by reason provided internal evidence for the validity of Christian revelation or that literary features of the gospel narratives, for example, their simplicity, were evidences for their historical reliability. Bushnell would seem to have tried to combine the "strengths" of both arguments. Character depiction itself becomes the single literary feature that evidences historicity. Yet in the final analysis the argument is not literary-historical at all. The God-man whom Bushnell constructs from the gospels has apologetical appeal only to those who share his vision of human perfection, who would wish but have failed to encounter it elsewhere, who consider it beyond human experience and human imagination.

That not only defenders but critics of historic Christianity share this vision is an assumption that Bushnell never questions, at least in *Nature and the Supernatural*. The few alleged "blemishes" that Parker and Hennell find in the character of Jesus are in Bushnell's opinion easily explained away: "should not a just reverence to one whose life is so nearly faultless, constrain us to look for some more favorable construction, that takes the solitary blemish away?"[14] Obviously this character sketch is not only a nineteenth-century ideal, but a nineteenth-century idealization. But in this respect Bushnell's work keeps company with many a nineteenth-century quester for the historical Jesus.

Perhaps Bushnell deserves some credit, however, for wrestling with the limitations of his own cultural bias. In *The Vicarious Sacrifice*, for example, he reconsidered the story, and this time he was troubled by its dissonance with modern bourgeois visions of perfection. In death, he notes, Christ is "a defeated and prostrate man, covered with unutterable ignominy."[15] In comparison with what the world expects of its great heroes, Christ is a riddle, "so that if we speak of heroes, we are tempted either to say that he is no hero at all, or else the only hero."[16] Now the resurrection alone is said to be able to revise one's impressions of him: "He becomes, at once, a wholly different being, whose life and death take, both, a wholly different meaning."[17] Revisionist interpretation of this sort does not prove that Bushnell had come to an improved reading of the gospels, but it does show that his hermeneutical sensors could on occasion detect disturbing elements in the biblical symbols.

In *Nature and the Supernatural* no such disturbances emerge. The

[14] Ibid., 328.
[15] Bushnell, *Vicarious Sacrifice*, 1:177.
[16] Ibid., 218.
[17] Ibid., 177, 205–12.

treatment accorded the "mythologic hypothesis" of Strauss is a case in point. The topic is taken up in Chapter XI, which deals with the question of the miracles of Jesus. The details of that discussion may be passed by here, except to note that Bushnell reverses the line of argument commonly advanced by eighteenth- and early nineteenth-century defenders of Christianity, including most evangelical and Unitarian thinkers of his time. He chooses to "prove" the miracles of Jesus by reference to the miracle of Jesus himself rather than to prove the divinity of Christ by reference to his miracles. In this regard he proceeds along a path already well traveled in Europe and soon to be followed by many other American liberals.

The credibility of the gospel accounts of miracles, however, is for Bushnell only a special instance of a credibility problem with the gospel "biographies" as a whole. Thus, he seeks to answer Strauss's claim that the miracle stories are "myths or legendary tales that grew up in the storytelling and marvelling habit of the disciples."[18] It is possible, Bushnell concedes, for history to be turned into fable over an extended period of time. But in dating the materials to the first thirty years after the death of Christ, Strauss does not allow enough time for such a development to occur. In order to accept his hypothesis, one would have to hold "that all these myths were developed and recorded in the lifetime of . . . the eye-witnesses themselves."[19] This, Bushnell concludes, is more incredible than the idea of miracles itself, especially since "the epistles, the genuineness of which is indisputable, present exactly the same Christ, and refer to the same miracles, in a manner clear of all pretense of myth or extravagance."[20]

To this argument is added another, which is basically a restatement of that already given in Chapter X. It challenges Parker's skeptical judgment that "we can learn few facts about Jesus,"[21] along with the hypothesis of Strauss. The bottom line is that the gospel picture of Jesus Christ could not be produced without a human model: "Nothing is so difficult, all human literature testifies, as to draw a character, and keep it in its living proportions. How much more to draw a perfect character, and not discolor it fatally by marks from the imperfection of the biographer. How is it, then, that four humble men, in an age of marvels and Rabbinical exaggerations, have done it?"[22] Bushnell will not argue that the evangelists were "infallible in their narrative," but since they produced an account of "the glorious, self-evidencing character of Jesus," it is unlikely that they would be unreliable about "simple matters of fact."[23]

---

18 Bushnell, *Nature and the Supernatural*, 355.
19 Ibid., 356.
20 Ibid.
21 Ibid., 358.
22 Ibid., 357.
23 Ibid., 358.

The worst that Bushnell will suppose on the question of historicity is that the gospels are mistaken "once, or twice" about details.[24]

Such scholarly, or more or less scholarly, arguments for the authenticity of the gospels and for the historicity of Christ were important to Bushnell. Yet they were clearly secondary to the proofs given when the gospels communicated the character of Christ to their readers and when the "organific power" of the God-man transformed human consciousness. Bushnell certainly held that it was only because of who Jesus was that such effects could come about. But it was only from these effects that the Christian received the higher assurance of faith regarding the identity of Jesus. Consequently, Bushnell's sermons and theological writings frequently dwelt upon the artistic expressiveness of the "incarnate biography" itself. His account of the work of Christ provides a good illustration of this concern.

[24] Ibid., 359.

VIII

GOD'S SAVING ART-WORK

Bushnell's conception of the theological task obliged him to give an account of the work of Christ that would be at once a comprehensive reading of biblical symbolism and an effective stimulus to the development of Christian religious awareness. It was an obligation he gladly, and tirelessly, tried to fulfill. Gladly, one can say, because the topic concerned what was in his judgment the essence of the gospel—that Jesus Christ transforms the human condition from life under sin to life in God. Tirelessly, one can say, because the difficulties of the task forced him to return to the topic again and again.[1]

Not the least of these difficulties was that of breaking through the impasse between orthodoxy and Unitarianism on the doctrine of the atonement. The orthodox argued among themselves over substitutionary, satisfaction, and governmental theories. But as a bloc they made common cause against the moral exemplar theory favored by the Unitarians. Bushnell saw in this protracted and often bitter dispute a fundamental disagreement over the end or aim of the mission of Jesus. Despite their in-house disagreements, the orthodox endorsed an "objective view" that conceived the work of Christ as effecting a change in God's dealings with sinful humanity. The Unitarians advocated a "subjective view" that conceived of the work as effecting a change in the disposition of sinful humanity toward God.[2] The problem, as Bushnell perceived it, was that neither the subjective nor the objective view could, by itself, comprehend the import of the biblical

---

[1] The train of thought is developed in Bushnell, "Revelation," 327–31; *God in Christ*, 119–81; *Christ in Theology*, 213–330; *Vicarious Sacrifice*, and *Forgiveness and Law*. The explanation of the "altar forms" of the Bible as objective representations of subjective experience is first stated in *God in Christ*, reaffirmed in *Christ in Theology*, and elaborated in *Vicarious Sacrifice*. Each presentation of the topic shows increased emphasis on the vicarious character of love, divine and human. The publication of *Forgiveness and Law* in 1874 was intended to replace Parts III and IV of *Vicarious Sacrifice*, for here the altar forms are taken to refer to the self-propitiating character of God's saving work in Jesus. At the same time, Bushnell emphasizes that the principles that ground the vicarious sacrifice are to be interpreted by the analogous experience of human interpersonal forgiveness.

[2] Bushnell, *God in Christ*, 203–5, 268–70. The options available for a doctrine of the atonement (subjective, objective, subjective–objective, and objective–subjective) are discussed in detail in *Christ in Theology*, 225–40.

record or link the atonement to the dynamics of sin and redemption known in human experience.

His own reflections on the impasse and the topic began with the acknowledgment that the Bible itself suggested both views.[3] Many passages clearly indicated that the work of Christ was designed to reconcile humanity to God. Yet many others contained terms and statements—"altar forms" of language such as sacrifice, offering, propitiation—which asserted some sort of transaction between the Son and the Father, independent of any human response to it. Thus, the conflict between orthodoxy and Unitarianism stemmed in part from one-sided, selective appeals to the range of biblical material on the subject. "The real problem," Bushnell maintained, "is to find a place and a meaning for *all* that is said concerning him [Christ]—to effect a union of the two sides."[4]

Lack of comprehensiveness was the one major criticism Bushnell had of both orthodoxy and Unitarianism. Lack of proper connection with the common thoughts and experiences of human nature was the other. The alleged weaknesses of orthodox positions in this regard had already been publicized by Unitarians, and Bushnell was in agreement with—and no doubt was influenced by—their arguments. In fastening on the objective view, Bushnell observed, orthodoxy "turns it into a dogma, and reasserts it as a theoretic or theologic truth."[5] But Bushnell denied that the dogma was a truth that thoughtful persons could accept. First, in subsuming the whole range of biblical symbols under one dominant judicial, commercial, or political analogy, orthodox theologians faced insurmountable problems in trying to relate justice and mercy, law and gospel, accountability and forgiveness. Second, they produced a picture of a God who demands the death of an innocent as a precondition for saving the guilty—a notion that "offends some right moral sentiment in humanity." Third, their description of a transaction between the persons of the Trinity failed to account for the transformation of human character brought about by the work of Christ.

In Bushnell's judgment one merit of the subjective view was that it avoided such problems by highlighting the moral power of God's saving action in Christ. Another was that it was true to the preponderant witness of the Bible on the topic. If one asks about the aim of Christ's mission, he wrote, "the answer of the scripture will be, that he comes to renovate character; to quicken by the infusion of the divine life; in one word, that he comes to be a Saviour, as saving his people from their sins."[6] Nonetheless, Bushnell found the moral exemplar theory of Unitarianism to

---

3 Bushnell, *God in Christ*, 189–90, 271.
4 Ibid., 190.
5 Ibid., 269.
6 Ibid., 191.

be an unsatisfactory account of the subjective view, because it could not deliver what it promised. The exemplary Christ models human perfection but does not enable persons to become what they are to be. In rejecting not only the objective theories of orthodoxy but the objective language of the Bible, Unitarianism preaches a dull and lifeless gospel. The altar forms in the Bible, Bushnell contends, have always had special power to sustain and to move the lives of "believers and martyrs." Without them Christianity becomes just another philosophy which instructs but does not renew.[7]

Bushnell's solution is to integrate the two views into a subjective-objective account, which speaks of Christ as a moral influence rather than as a moral example.[8] In order to "reclaim and restore" the objective language of the Bible, it is necessary to recognize that the subjective aim of Christ's mission "could not be effectively realized, without the second, or objective view, in which his whole work is conceived in the altar form, and held forth to the objective embrace and worship and response of faith."[9] The blending of the two views within the Bible itself is to be read as an artistically puissant whole:

> It is more a poem than a treatise. It classes as a work of Art more than as a work of Science. It addresses the understanding, in great part, through the feeling or sensibility. In these it has its receptivities, by these it is perceived, or perceivable. Moving in and through these, as a revelation of sympathy, love, life, it proposes to connect us with the Life of God.[10]

The blending of the two views within theology is therefore to be sensitive to the peculiar expressive power of biblical language. And since the meaning of art cannot be exhausted by a simple formula or summary, a doctrine of the atonement will be akin to a literary criticism designed to increase one's appreciation of the story.[11]

The story of Jesus' life, teachings, and death is to find its meaning in its tragic force. Here the reader encounters "the highest and most moving tragedy ever acted in this mortal sphere; a tragedy distinguished in the fact that God is the Chief Character, and the divine feeling, moved in tragic earnest—Goodness Infinite manifested through Sorrow—the passion represented."[12] As an event in history, the tragedy has "an organific power" to transform human consciousness. As a literary story it has the power to bring readers to remorse for sin and, "then, when God appears in His beauty, loving and lovely, the good, the glory, the sunlight

[7] Ibid., 203, 261–63.
[8] Ibid., 192; idem, *Christ in Theology*, 238–40.
[9] Bushnell, *God in Christ*, 192.
[10] Ibid., 204.
[11] Ibid.
[12] Ibid., 204–5.

of soul, the affections, previously dead, wake into life and joyful play, and what before was only a self-lifting and slavish effort becomes an exulting spirit of liberty."[13]

The reference to the beauty of God in Christ calls to mind what Bushnell evidently deems to be among the chief benefits of the type of biblical reading he recommends. It made possible a fresh understanding of terms that had been killed off by the doctrinal tradition. In his sermon "The Word Grace Revived," for example, he attempts to restore meaning to the word by this means.[14] His introductory comments sum up his concern:

> It is with words often as with men, they are mortal, they die. They are used loosely and subjected to such abuses that the life of their meaning perishes. Exactly this has been the portion of the Scripture word, *grace*. It has been so roughly handled in the wear of theology, subjected to so many artificial strains of construction, and used with so great ardor while losing its intelligent meaning, that finally its life has gone quite out. . . . Originally one of the liveliest and most beautiful words, it is now virtually lost to us, it is a dead word. And yet in the Scripture it is the vital, central word of Christian experience itself.[15]

From word usage common to both classical and New Testament Greek, he concludes that "the key to the real living meaning of the word" rests with its sensory reference to "beauty in person and action, as when we speak of graceful manners or bearing."[16] In the Bible, this first-level order of signification has been transferred to the realm of spiritual truth by associating physical attractiveness with "a spirit of benignity and favor."[17]

It is this meaning, Bushnell claims, that is suggested when biblical texts apply the word "grace" to God, to the life and death of Jesus, and to the terms of salvation.[18] "It [grace] was not designed to raise some very exact metaphysical or legal distinction between justice and mercy. It only conceived in God something more winning, free and gracious than mere authority or vindicative justice or a sturdy adherence of will to his own terms of commandment, and calls it by a fit contrast the grace of God in Jesus Christ."[19] As a poetic form expressive of Christian experience, grace is used to testify that God has attracted, charmed, and drawn the self into union with the divine. Thus the term is properly employed in contemporary theology when it serves to connect the work

13 Ibid., 212–13.
14 Bushnell, "The Word Grace Revived," *Spirit in Man*, 262–70.
15 Ibid., 262.
16 Ibid., 263–64.
17 Ibid., 265.
18 Ibid., 265–66.
19 Ibid., 267.

of Christ in the past with the work of Christ in the present.

It is in just this way that Bushnell seeks to reclaim the altar forms of the Bible. Their first-order level of meaning has been instituted by God in order to provide "metaphors of new salvation when it should come."[20] Their presence in the New Testament, and hence in the theological tradition, results from a transference of the literal meanings to symbolic usage expressive of Christian experience.

> These forms are the objective equivalents of our subjective impressions. Indeed, our impressions have their life and power in and under these forms. Neither let it be imagined that we only happen to seize upon these images of sacrifice, atonement, and blood, because they are at hand. They are prepared, as God's form of art, for the representation of Christ and his work; and if we refuse to let him pass into this form, we have no mold of thought that can fitly represent him.[21]

In short, their introduction into Christology is warranted, indeed required, as an effort at symbolic communication. And only because of a dogged literalism have both the orthodox and the Unitarians failed to appreciate their meaning.

Bushnell argues, further, that the altar forms are indispensable to the artistic power of the gospel. The use of such objective statements, he maintains, is by no means unusual. There is a "mental instinct" that leads persons to express their feelings and thoughts in such terms: "Thus we say of a scene, that it was *pitiful*, or *joyful*, or *delightful*, not because the scene itself was really full of pity, joy, or delight, but because we were so ourselves."[22] In religion the instinct is always operative—manifested in the external rites and vocabulary of worship. In both cases, the value of objective forms is that they impress themselves with special force upon the sensibilities.

In the Christian religion, he contends, they play not this role but an even more important one. By depicting the saving work of Jesus Christ as something accomplished outside of the human self, the altar forms of the Bible draw readers away from themselves and from their own efforts at self-culture. "And precisely here is the fundamental necessity of an objective form or forms of art, in the Christian scheme. While a man is addressing his own nature with means, motives, and remedies, . . . he is very certainly held to that which he needs most of all to escape, viz., the hinging of his life on himself; and the interests of his own person."[23] Altar forms, then, are necessary for a religious experience in which "we

---

[20] Bushnell, "Our Gospel A Gift," *Building Eras in Religion*, 254.
[21] Bushnell, *God in Christ*, 254.
[22] Ibid., 246.
[23] Ibid., 263.

are carried off our own centre that God may fix our orbit for us about Himself."[24] In a manner of "Divine Art" the objectivity of the expressions helps produce the very experience from which it has arisen.

In sum, Bushnell's moral influence "theory" of the atonement is not meant to be a construction but a recollection of the significatory power of biblical symbols. It is not to replace but to capitalize on what he sees as an artful complementarity of subjective and objective language. By his account the work of Christ, which occurs as an event in the past and is depicted in a text from the past, becomes in the engagement between the text and its reader a work that extends into the present.

The point of contact between the text and the reader, according to Bushnell, is a common experience—suffering love. In this he finds the natural analogy that "grafts in" the biblical symbols upon human life. Experience testifies, he maintains, that a broken relationship requires an initiatory and abiding love that will neither tolerate nor overlook injury but will bear with the transgressor in order to bring about reconciliation. "Love," he explains, "is a principle essentially vicarious in its own nature, identifying the subject with others, so as to suffer their adversities and pains, and taking on itself the burden of their evils."[25] So it is that the love of God in Christ suffers the cross in order to awaken the dormant receptivity of the human self: "Vicarious love in him answered by vicarious love in us, tiny and weak though it be, as an insect life fluttering responsively to the sun—this is the only footing of grace, in which Christ is truly received, and according to his glorious power."[26]

Here Bushnell breaks with the dominant options in New England theology, with their appeals to judicial, governmental, and didactic analogies for the work of Christ. But as Conrad Cherry has perceptively noted, the break was by no means complete: "Like theologians from Dwight to Taylor to Channing, he measured God by a general principle common to God and creature. For Bushnell that principle was not harmony, duty, happiness, or disinterested commitment to law, it was love, suffering love."[27] Within Bushnell's theology, this principle vindicated God's perfection by identifying a standard of goodness common to God and humanity. True, care was taken to emphasize that the standard was internal, not external, to the Godhead. But if forced to choose between the inscrutability and the communicability of God, Bushnell was inclined to opt for the latter.

Viewed in the context of his theory of biblical interpretation, the principle raises more than a single issue. Cherry faults Bushnell for

---

[24] Ibid., 265.

[25] Bushnell, *Vicarious Sacrifice*, 1:42.

[26] Ibid., 124.

[27] Cherry, *Nature and Religious Imagination*, 182.

inconsistency: "in making suffering love a general principle, he speculated behind the symbol to a non-symbolic, universal standard of excellence."[28] The point is well taken, for Bushnell's appreciation of the inexhaustible, productive indeterminacy of symbol is evidently overwhelmed by his desire for an account of the work of Christ that is intelligible, and acceptable, to nineteenth-century sensibilities. "Here, then, is our first point, when we attempt the cross and sacrifice of Christ; we must bring every thing back under the common standards of eternal virtue. . . . That which is to be intelligible must be found within the bounds of intelligence. If we can not find a Saviour under just our laws of good, we shall find him nowhere."[29] This ascent into meaning is a trip with only one predetermined destination.

In *Forgiveness and Law* the analogical connection between symbol and its meaning—always mysterious—becomes utterly baffling. Here Bushnell refers to "the grand analogy or *almost identity* that subsists between our moral nature and that of God" adding that "he [God] is brought so close to us that *almost any thing* that occurs in the workings or exigencies of our moral instincts may even be expected in his."[30] As the discussion proceeds, the analogy in fact becomes an identity: the moral instincts of God correspond fully to those of humanity.

What is remarkable about this move, however, is that it allows Bushnell to alter a position he had taken in *The Vicarious Sacrifice*:

> I asserted a propitiation before, but accounted for the word as one by which the disciple objectivizes his own feeling, conceiving that God is representatively mitigated or become propitious, because he is himself inwardly reconciled to God. Instead of this, I now assert a real propitiation of God, finding it in evidence from the propitiation we instinctively make ourselves when we heartily forgive.[31]

This was a "conservative" opinion that impressed neither the orthodox nor the liberals of his day. Bushnell "rescued" an imperiled symbol. But the cost was high: the term forgiveness carried a univocal, not a symbolic, meaning.

The revised estimate of the word propitiation in *Forgiveness and Law* at the same time illustrates another way in which the tension at the heart of his hermeneutical theory works out in practice. The explicative meanings of the altar forms in the Bible are clearly found in what they suggest about the life of God, but in seeking to merge explicative and applicative meaning Bushnell must limit his account to what can be appropriated into human life. Thus application becomes not merely the culmination but the

---

[28] Ibid., 183.
[29] Bushnell, *Vicarious Sacrifice*, 1:58.
[30] Bushnell, *Forgiveness and Law*, 35 (emphasis added).
[31] Ibid., 12.

norm of interpretation. This was a possibility, a danger, inherent in his conception of dialogical communication. In combating the tendency, common among both dogmatic and historical interpreters, to allow explication to dominate application, Bushnell here shifts to the opposite extreme and allows application to dominate explication.

IX

FROM EXEGESIS TO HOMILETICS

The supreme test of Bushnell's biblical studies came with the sermon. The cultural situation virtually dictated as much. So long as Protestantism held sway in education and in civic discussion, it kept biblical scholarship, doctrinal theology, and homiletical arts in a roundelay. The movements of each member of the threesome varied, but the dance went on without interruption. In Bushnell's case the lead fell to homiletics, at least with respect to his priorities and his reputation. No appraisal of his contribution to biblical scholarship can gainsay the primacy of preaching in his career.

Homiletics gained its lead only gradually. Bushnell's qualms about preaching lingered long after his doubts about the truth of Christianity had vanished. In time, however, he came to find gratification in this aspect of his work, and after retiring from North Church he relished the opportunity to preach and to publish his sermons.[1] Status-seeking had a hand in this, but the development proceeded by an almost implacable logic. If the essence of Christianity depended on a dialectic between the biblical rhetoric of revelation and the socially shaped consciousness of the individual, he could hardly shrink from the challenge of making the "biblical message" a vital force at the front line where the preacher met the public. Here, above all, a study of the Bible would have to yield dividends.

Bushnell's social set during "the golden age of American oratory" prized neither a Puritan plain style nor an emotional harangue.[2] Its homiletical ideal came from the lyceum: edification and inspiration through eloquence. The guidance that would-be preachers got from Bushnell was fully compatible with the ideal. They were told to gain an appreciation

---

[1] A psychological interpretation of the biographical data is offered by Cross, *Horace Bushnell*, chap. 6. A letter of 19 June 1862 illustrates Bushnell's attitude toward preaching in retirement: "As my old pulpit is now vacant, I am trying to put in a sermon a week there. How long I shall stand so much, I don't know. I could go on to the world's end, or to mine, for there is nothing I so much delight in as preaching" (Cheyney, *Life and Letters*, 478).

[2] Edward Parker, *The Golden Age of American Oratory* (Boston: Whittemore, Niles, and Hall, 1857). On Bushnell, see Cross, *Horace Bushnell*, chap. 6; and Thompson, *Changing Emphases in American Preaching*.

for people and for the gospel by contemplating the "dignities, and powers, and forthcoming glories of souls" and by "beholding their uplifting
of stature in the new divine life which is called their salvation."[3] The
"four canonical talents" cultivated in the seminary classroom—high
scholarship, metaphysical and thinking talent, talent for expression or
style, and talent of manner and voice for speaking—were not to be
ignored.[4] At the same time, "a disproportionate interest in the direction
of speculative theology" was singled out as the occupational hazard to be
avoided at any cost.[5]

Crucial to effective preaching, Bushnell maintained, was the "indi-
vidualizing talent" for speaking in specific, indeed, quite personalized,
terms.[6] "True preaching struggles right away from formula, back into
fact, and life, and the revelation of God and heaven. It is a flaming out
from God; it reproves, testifies, calls, promises. . . ."[7] Such discourse
obviously required more than erudition and a gift of gab. What Bushnell
had in mind was a sound knowledge of human nature and a "mysterious
efflux" and "aerial development of one's personality."[8] The sermon was
to evidence learning and craft, but even more it was to be "momentum
of private inspirations: that which makes a man a symbol, and a voice,
and a power."[9]

This advice was in line not only with the tastes of the upwardly mobile
middle classes but with an emerging consensus that preaching should bring
the Bible directly to bear on the cross-currents of everyday life and that the
"truth" to be communicated, be it the shock of regenerative grace or the
call of the sensitized conscience, should issue forth from the depths of the
speaker's soul. Bushnell had no cause to contest this view. A Christianity
that was Life and Spirit would surely produce sermons that evinced the life
and spirit of the preacher. And since exegesis was a process of "discovery"
through imaginative engagement, the sermon that announced that discovery would thereby initiate the process anew among its listeners. In this
sense preaching was to be exegesis in action. This placed heavy demands
on Bushnell the preacher. As Barbara Cross keenly observed, "if he disdained and avoided any foolish inconsistency, he exacted an unfailing originality of himself. Of the two, the latter obligation may have been the more
burdensome."[10] Burdensome or not, it was part of the ideal that Bushnell
did his utmost to approximate.

---

3 Horace Bushnell, "Training for the Pulpit Manward," *Building Eras in Religion*, 244.
4 Horace Bushnell, "Pulpit Talent," *Building Eras in Religion*, 185–93.
5 Bushnell, "Training for the Pulpit Manward," 226.
6 Bushnell, "Pulpit Talent," 196–98.
7 Ibid., 188.
8 Ibid., 193–207.
9 Bushnell,"Training for the Pulpit Manward." 244–45.
10 Cross, *Horace Bushnell*, 87.

It is bootless to debate how "great" a preacher he was. "A minor master of oratory and didactic prose" is the nicely phrased judgment of David Smith.[11] Many earlier commentators, however, have been lavish in their praise. Tribute has been paid him for freshness, originality, reach of thought, and spiritual sentiment; for inventing striking titles; for making much of hitherto unpromising verses; for attending to the "moral system of the universe"; for "that direct contact with human spirits."[12] G. S. Drew claimed, "his sermons can never be burdened with the common reproach of sermons, that they are unpractical"; and here even the common reproach that burdened his scholarship proved to redound to his credit, for "the tendency to exaggerate some one element of truth, and to let it for the moment eclipse correlated elements of equal moment" was said to enhance his sermons.[13] Nor did "the mysterious efflux" and "aerial development" of his personality pass unnoticed. Nelson Beach included him among those "transcendental preachers" who seemed "to dwell all the time in the presence of the world unseen."[14] If no one hastened to set him above the Beechers, *père et fils*, or Brooks, Maurice, Robertson, or Spurgeon, there was no hesitation about calling him their peer.[15] All told, such extravagant praise identifies an unusual preacher, the practical visionary.

The encomiasts may be spared cross-examination. Their testimony serves only to corroborate the obvious—Bushnell's thought and the biblical study behind it were widely disseminated through his sermons. As Fisher put it, "on his contemporaries, at least, Dr. Bushnell's sermons will exert an influence excelled by that of few preachers of the time."[16] No less obvious is the fact that Bushnell's sermons are of such a nature that the path from exegesis to homiletics—rarely smooth and direct in any case—is singularly difficult to trace. Bushnell was not an exegetical or

---

[11] D. L. Smith, *Symbolism and Growth*, viii.

[12] G. S. Drew, "An American Divine: Horace Bushnell," *Contemporary Review* 35 (1879) 829; Henry M. Goodwin, "Dr. Bushnell's Sermons for the New Life," *New Englander* 17 (1859) 385; Theodore Munger, *Horace Bushnell: Preacher and Theologian* (Boston: Houghton, Mifflin, 1899) 285, 187–88; Austin Phelps, *The Theory of Preaching: Lectures on Homiletics* (New York: Charles Scribner's Sons, 1891) 61; Henry C. Sheldon, *The History of the Christian Church* (New York and Boston: Thomas Y. Crowell, 1894) 5:226–27.

[13] G. P. Fisher, "Horace Bushnell," *International Review* 10 (1881) 24; Goodwin, "Dr. Bushnell's Sermons," 288–92; J. M. Hoppin, "Bushnell's *Sermons on Living Subjects*," *New Englander* 31 (1873) 99.

[14] David Nelson Beach, *A Handbook of Homiletics* (Bangor: John H. Bacon, 1912) 136–39, 149.

[15] Benjamin Wisner Bacon, *Theodore Thornton Munger: New England Minister* (New Haven: Yale University Press; London: Humphrey Milford/Oxford University, 1913) 271; Beach, *Handbook of Homiletics*, 153–68; Drew, "An American Divine," 828–29; Munger, *Horace Bushnell*, 271.

[16] Fisher, "Horace Bushnell," 24.

expository preacher. If his sermons exhibit his exegetical research, it is not because they expound scholarly conclusions but because they deploy biblical symbols with some regard for their aesthetic force.

A case in point would be Bushnell's interpretation of Pauline materials and, in particular, some of those that had propped up the doctrine of justification by grace through faith. The cloud of Protestant witnesses surrounding him regarded this doctrine as the gospel *in nuce*. Like other Reformed theologians (and was he not?), Bushnell might be expected to search here for the link between biblical revelation and experimental piety. What makes his interest in this theme so intriguing, however, is that he was repelled by the traditional image of Paul.

That image—Paul the dogmatician—seemed to confront him at every turn. So long as the orthodox could lay claim to *the* Apostle, the prospects for the type of theological renewal that Bushnell aimed at were doubtful. The "logic-choppers," Bushnell believed, had created a Paul in their own image—a propounder of unvarnished (literal) truth about the placation of divine wrath, forensic grace, and imputed righteousness, all in accord with divine decrees. To one who wanted "'more light to break forth from God's holy word'—not from the formulas, or the catechisms, or the schools, or the doctors, but from God's holy word; and especially from those parts of the word which represent the Christian truth as spirit and as life,"[17] the epistles of Paul the dogmatist were hardly inviting resources.

Bushnell's fondness for the gospels, and for John's gospel above all, reflects his desire to expand the canon within the canon. But as tempting as it may have been to play Paul off against Jesus or to avoid Paul entirely, Bushnell refused to surrender Paul's epistles to the dogmatists. If, as he sincerely believed, New England theology had lost the true gospel about "Christ the manifested life,"[18] the loss was to be overcome by correcting traditional misreadings of Paul. The basic problem with that reading, he thought, was that between the two points, justification and spirit, the manifestation of Jesus Christ as an active force was lacking.[19] At the one point, justification was conceived "too literally" along judicial lines,[20] and as a result the work of Christ was set in a tribunal above and beyond the realm of Christian experience. At the other point, the spirit was conceived as though it were an "abstract and dry agency—mere efficiency, running out of the divine decrees," unrelated to social, moral

[17] Here Bushnell cites, and "applies," a remark by John Robinson (Bushnell, *God in Christ*, 297).
[18] Bushnell, *Christ in Theology*, 218–20.
[19] Ibid., 220–21.
[20] Bushnell, *God in Christ*, 344–45.

relations, without influence on us.[21] Overlooked was the Paul who proclaimed that the gospel is the presence and power of Christ operative in the life of the believer.

Remolding the image of Paul was a major undertaking that demanded effort at several points. It was necessary to show that Paul's language was creative, symbolic, and unsystematic. At the same time it was important to restore the "true Pauline gospel" contained in 1 Corinthians 2, where "Christianity is a ministration of the spirit."[22] And emphasis was due on the word "esthetic" so that the meaning of Philippians 1:9–10 could emerge, for there the Christian religion is represented "as a power moving upon man, through this department of his nature, both to regenerate his degraded perception of excellence, and also to communicate in that way the fullness and beauty of God."[23]

Extensive consideration was given to Romans 3:25–26, a standard text for orthodox accounts of justification: "Whom God hath set forth to be a propitiation, through faith in his blood, to declare his righteousness, for the remission of sins that are past, through the forbearance of God; to declare, I say, at this time his righteousness, that he might be just, and the justifier of him which believeth in Jesus."[24] In this passage Bushnell sought exegetical evidence to counter the traditional claims of orthodoxy. The main points of his analysis can be briefly summarized.

The most puzzling aspect of the text has to do with the relationship between the concepts propitiation on the one hand and justification on the other. Neither Roman Catholic nor Protestant interpreters have successfully solved the puzzle, for in their zealous quest for conceptual consistency they have compromised the righteousness of God. New possibilities emerge, however, when the key terms in the passage are viewed not as concepts, but as metaphors carried over into Christianity from its Jewish background.

> The doctrine of Christ, prepared in the terms of the altar service, has no strictly historic connection with the doctrine of Christ, asserted under the form of justification. The two doctrines, distinct in form and the historic origin of their symbols, are only *coincident* in their general substance. One is priestly in its form and origin, the other stands in symbols derived from law and governmental order, and is more nearly political and speculative in its form.[25]

The *Sitz im Leben* for these two ways of speaking was the Jewish schools, where the Sadducees, "the Unitarians of the day," and the Pharisees, the

---

21 Ibid., 349.
22 Ibid., 291.
23 Ibid., 204.
24 Bushnell, *Forgiveness and Law*, 177.
25 Bushnell, *Christ in Theology*, 268.

defenders of mosaic orthodoxy, debated what made a person acceptable in God's sight. The former maintained that one is justified by becoming just and righteous; the other, by adhering to the letter of the law. In his own teaching, Jesus rejected both alternatives and claimed that eternal life hinged on a decision of faith for or against him.[26]

According to Bushnell, Paul's use of the two metaphors was in continuity with the self-proclamation of Jesus. By drawing upon language of ritual sacrifice, he underscored that the changed relationship between God and humanity is effected by the life and death of Jesus, that God is the active agent in this change, and that the actuality of this new relationship is known only in and by faith.[27] The one "set forth to be a propitiation" is the one whose entire ministry "expresses" and "impresses" itself upon the individual, through that mode of apprehension called faith.[28] The repetition of the word *endeixis* confirms as much, for the declaration is, "literally," an "in-showing" of the righteousness of God within the world and within the consciousness of the believer. Thus, the "divinely great character of Jesus Christ" demonstrates that God is righteousness in his excellence to make righteous those who believe.[29]

There is an implied parallelism between the two clauses of the statement that deserves attention. "The term *justification*, here, answers indeed to the term *remission*, there, as nearly as a political or judicial symbol can, to a priestly or ritual."[30] Like the altar term, the word justification has its objective and subjective sides, God's acquittal and human regeneration. The import of the passage, however, is misinterpreted when the one side is emphasized at the expense of the other. On this matter Tholuck and "other [unnamed] distinguished theologians of Germany" are agreed. In his *Commentary on Romans*, Tholuck observes that "the expositors who seized, exclusively, on the one or the other view, have never been able to arrive at perfect perspicuity."[31] A nonreductionist interpretation, then, will extend the parallelism. Just as a formal judgment of forgiveness is nothing until it is carried out by "a subjective deliverance" from the power of sin, so an objective justification is nothing until it is carried out "in the soul and character, an inward actual deliverance."[32] Although Tholuck himself grants a certain priority to the objective side, it is not a temporal or sequential *prius* that leaves the subjective side in abeyance. The passage implies both sides; the two ways of speaking will "coalesce in a consistent and common result" if the

---

26 Ibid., 268–69.
27 Bushnell, *Forgiveness and Law*, 72–73.
28 Bushnell, *Christ in Theology*, 273.
29 Bushnell, *Forgiveness and Law*, 177–78.
30 Bushnell, *Christ in Theology*, 288.
31 Ibid., 293.
32 Ibid., 288.

objective side is said to be known only in the subjective.[33] Paul is speaking of "a righteousness *unto and upon* all; upon as being unto; unto that it may be upon, transferred as being imputed; imputed that it may be transferred," and thus the phrase "Christ our righteousness" takes on here an "instrumental or experiential" value pertaining to a justification of and in life.[34]

Support for this line of interpretation comes from a look at the terms *dikaiosynē, dikaios,* and *dikaiounta.* Although all three words are derived from a common root, students of the English Bible have been misled (unconscionably, Bushnell thinks) by the translators who substitute two sets of words for those in the passage—the "Saxon" terms "right/righteousness" and the Latin terms "just/justify." Since the Latin *jus* will bear either a legal meaning related to "the penal redress of crimes" or a moral meaning related "wholly to character," the result in English (and by implication in the Vulgate) has been "a jumble of ambiguities." A survey of Greek word usage, however, confirms that the Greek root always occurs in the context of moral discourse. If it were possible, then, to "get rid of these Latin-born terms," it would become clear that "the sense of scripture" is that the passage is to be interpreted in moral rather than forensic terms.[35]

Bushnell's exegetical homework on this passage will not withstand twentieth-century scrutiny, and one may even look wistfully at a bygone moment when momentous questions about Pauline thought could be handled without confronting the topic of eschatology at all. The objections that Bushnell anticipated would come from his contemporaries were those that arose from misplaced confessional commitments. Thus a special effort was made to demonstrate that this reading comported fully with the heritage of the reformation. "Justification is not to be conceived as an accomplished fact, as indeed it never can be, prior to faith in the subject."[36] This, Bushnell insisted, was the insight that Luther had discovered in his heart. But, unfortunately, "his heart sailed over his theology and did not come down to see it," for when he turned to articulate the insight he often relapsed into scholastic categories.[37] Like the pre-Reformation schoolmen, those who incorporated this insight into dogmatic theology misunderstood "the objective figures and free metaphors of the bible."[38] Whereas Roman Catholicism produced a doctrine of justification that was "vicious" because it implied that human beings can attain a righteousness apart from faith, Protestantism produced a "defective" doctrine that was "too rigid and

[33] Ibid., 295–96.
[34] Ibid., 313–14.
[35] Bushnell, *Forgiveness and Law*, 177–80.
[36] Ibid., 204.
[37] Ibid., 208.
[38] Bushnell, *Christ in Theology*, 310.

speculative, as being a transaction external to us."[39] True orthodoxy—"the experimental, never-to-be-antiquated, Scripture truth of imputed righteousness"[40] will be that a right relationship to God comes about when the divine righteousness made manifest in Jesus Christ is made manifest as well in the life of the individual Christian.

To what homiletical use was such exegesis put? A Bushnell sermon on Romans 3:25–26 is not available, but it is not hard to find out how Bushnell preached the gospel of "justification." A good example is "The Putting on of Christ," which as the title indicates, is based on Romans 13:41, "but put ye on the Lord Jesus Christ." From start to finish Bushnell plays on the figure of speech embedded in this exhortation.

The message begins abruptly: "The highest distinction of man, taken as an animal among animals, lies not in his two-handedness, or his erect figure, but in his necessity and right of dress." Unlike the "clothing" worn by animals, which grows by necessity, that worn by the human creature betokens a "superior dignity" and a "really high prerogative"— the freedom to exhibit outwardly the "quality" of personal character. With such liberty, however, comes peril, for the manner of dress may be only a mask for raw ambition, and thus "under sin" this mark of distinction becomes "a mighty instigator in the fearful race of money, society, and fashion."[41]

The clue to Paul's meaning is the habitual association of outward appearance and inward character—an association, it can be presumed, familiar enough to modern Yankees. Dress is "the outward analagon, or figure of character, and of character as the grand 'putting on' of the soul." The frequent use of the analogy in the Bible—"the wedding garment," "the robe of righteousness," "white raiment," "filthiness in the skirts," "clothed with salvation"—needs to be mentioned only in passing. Such references do prepare the reader, however, for the meaning of the Romans text. Since "whatever has power to produce a character when received, is represented as a dress to be put on," Paul too can admonish his readers to put on Jesus Christ as the dress of their souls.[42]

The pertinence of the analogy for "the great problem of life as a moral and spiritual affair" is illustrated by the story of the "old Adam" and Eve. The "fig-leaf history" of their fall graphically depicts the "shock" to their innocence, their loss of character, and their shame as an awareness of a nakedness or lack of covering. As soon as the "investiture of God" is stripped from them, they resort to makeshift garments in order to disguise their loss. Their story is a paradigm of human history.

[39] Ibid., 314–15.
[40] Bushnell, *Forgiveness and Law*, 214.
[41] Horace Bushnell, "The Putting on of Christ," *Christ and His Salvation*, 413–14.
[42] Ibid., 414–15.

Lacking genuine self-respect, persons ceaselessly hide behind the mere appearance of dignity. Politeness, honors, bravery, sacrifices to idols, self-torture, penances, vows of abstinence and poverty, exactness in rites and traditions, orthodoxy, almsgiving, honesty in trade, works of reform, and philanthropy are among their outward displays.[43]

Paul's message is about a quite different "covering"; it concerns the righteousness of God revealed in Christ to faith. To be robed in Christ is to be infolded in God; "the incovering beauty of God's own feeling and Spirit," which had "enveloped" Adam, is offered once again to all who are in Christ.[44] It was for this purpose that Christ was sent forth into the world. His "atonement" is, "literally," a "covering," and sinful humanity is "covered" by Christ inasmuch as Christ "copies himself into us, to be our righteousness of God upon us."[45] The incarnation itself is a "humanizing" of God: the divine draws toward humanity so that humanity will be drawn toward, and into, the divine.[46] Apart from such a manifestation, the "very perfections of God . . . would be only impassive, distant, autocratic, and it may be, even repulsive, as they often are, in the teachings now of Christian theology."[47] Those teachings are apparently too well known to require specification.

The work of Christ may be understood in light of its effects, and like Melanchthon and Schleiermacher before him, Bushnell preaches that one should know Christ through his benefits. The gospel is that "we are to be new-charactered, by the putting on of Christ. . . . Christ is to be a complete wardrobe for himself." It is in this sense that the phrase "righteousness of faith" is to be understood: "Christ is everything for us and upon us."[48] To put on Christ is, first, to put aside the world, "the lusts of property, and fame, and power, and appetite."[49] It is, second, to experience the presence of Christ as a regenerative power which works to "assimilate" all that one is to all that Christ was.[50] This is "sanctification," for the "vestiges of disease, and disorder, and bad passion" are replaced by a "superinduced character of beauty."[51] And it is, third, to receive "a new consciousness of strength and exalted confidence of feeling" that makes believers "Christophers, Christ-bearers."[52]

[43] Ibid., 415–18.
[44] Ibid., 419.
[45] Ibid., 420.
[46] Ibid., 421.
[47] Ibid., 431.
[48] Ibid., 422–23.
[49] Ibid., 426.
[50] Ibid., 427.
[51] Ibid., 428–29.
[52] Ibid., 431.

Since "the one true salvation-title is Christ put on," Bushnell admonishes the congregation to beware of works righteousness. "A great many persons are at work, in these times," he says, "to fashion a character for themselves and demanding it of them who preach the gospel that they preach conduct, tell men how to be good and right, correct their faults, make them good husbands, wives, children, citizens—cease, in a word, from the mystic matter of faith and divine experience, and put the world on doing something more solid and satisfactory."[53] This, of course, is a misguided, half-way measure, for what is needed is not merely, or initially, improved conduct, but "a new man."[54] The parable of the wedding feast is cited to illustrate the point: "it will not suffice to wrap oneself in the robe of self-criticism, self-endeavor, and self-righteousness." The true wedding garment is Christ. Here is the "fearfully precise point on which eternity hinges. . . . We must put on Christ himself, and none but him. We must be in-Christed."[55]

In concluding, Bushnell returns to the theme of the righteousness of God.

> Far be it also from us, when we put on Christ, to think of turning ourselves about, in the search for some other, finer, pretext that we may put on over him, to make him attractive, pleasing, acceptable. No, we are to put him on just as he is, wear him outside, walk in him, bear his reproach, glory in his beauty, call it good to die with him, so to be found in him not having our own righteousness, but the righteousness that is of God by faith. Cover us in it, O Thou Christ of God, and let our shame be hid eternally in thee.[56]

If this sermon is not Bushnell's finest, it is nevertheless, and perhaps for that very reason, quite exemplary. In terms of its form, it is structured, but neither fully disciplined nor proportioned. Its style and tone befit classic nineteenth-century oratory, even though sometimes the wit (e.g., a "fig-leaf history") and the turn-of-phrase (e.g., "in-Christed") are a touch baroque. The content itself is vintage Bushnell. Justification is not so much defined and unpacked as it is described in light of its psychological, if not existential, ramifications. The transition from the Old Adam to the New is known, that is, experienceable and discussable, as a transformation of "character." In order to distinguish, but not to separate, character as a state of being and as a series of acts, Bushnell challenges works-righteousness in sweet-and-sour language. In contrast to some of his sermons, this one provides only an exasperatingly vague account of the shape of the regenerate life. It provides instead an

53 Ibid., 431–32.
54 Ibid., 432.
55 Ibid., 432–33.
56 Ibid., 433.

emphatic, even tendentious, insistence on the "essential" point—union with Christ.

Bushnell's imaginative engagement with this text is without doubt more than Paul would have bargained for.[57] Yet the image of "putting on a garment" proves to be eminently exploitable. As an alternative to a forensic model, it reduces the distance between a judge and a defendant, and the use of synonyms, such as "enveloped" and "infolded" suggests both the objectivity and the intimacy of the atonement. Of course, the image does have its limits. To ask whether "the clothes make the man" or "the clothes express the man" would be to separate the objective and subjective sides of justification. And at crucial junctures Bushnell must shift from talking about the "infolding" of Christ to talking about the "in-dwelling" of Christ. After all, he had warned that a single image gives only a partial glimpse of truth. The Pauline epistles, he thought, emphasize not only life "in Christ" but also "Christ in us."

The sermon, like Bushnell's exegetical homework, replaces the dogmatic Paul with a Paul who seizes upon symbols in order to suggest the dynamics of sin and grace. In a sense, then, Paul is truly a theologian, that is, an expositor of Christian consciousness, *because* he is a poet—preacher. The center of the Pauline message is not a "speculative" doctrine of imputed justification but an experiential testimony to communion with Christ. Bushnell would not go so far as to say that justification is "a subsidiary crater" in Pauline theology,[58] but he is determined to interpret that theme in the context of a "real" presence of Christ in the believer. Thus, "the mysticism of Paul the Apostle" appears in Bushnell's sermons before it enters decisively into the scholarship of New England biblical specialists.

---

[57] See, e.g., K. Kertelge, *"Rechtfertigung" bei Paulus* (Münster: Aschendorff, 1967); and J. A. Ziesler, *The Meaning of Righteousness in Paul: A Linguistic and Theological Inquiry* (Cambridge: Cambridge University, 1972).

[58] Albert Schweitzer, *The Mysticism of Paul the Apostle*, trans. W. Montgomery (New York: Macmillan, 1951, c. 1931) 225. Discussions of the history of modern Pauline interpretation are available in Albert Schweitzer, *Paul and his Interpreters: A Critical History* (New York: Schocken, 1964); C. Müller, *Gottes Gerechtigkeit und Gottes Volk* (Göttingen: Vandenhoeck & Ruprecht 1964); Peter Stuhlmacher, *Gerechtigkeit Gottes bei Paulus* (Göttingen: Vandenhoeck & Ruprecht, 1966).

EPILOGUE

Bushnell died in 1876, just as American Christianity entered "a critical period" in its development.[1] During his lifetime the academy and the church had their first brush with modern biblical scholarship. The results had been unsettling but perhaps "containable." In his *Recollections*, Washington Gladden wrote that even in 1875 Congregationalist ministers were loathe to speak openly of the new criticism, and Benjamin Wisner Bacon's memory of the situation at Yale Divinity School of 1881 was much the same.[2] The encounter with lower and higher criticism had been so limited, and within the evangelical camps so tentative, that the very acceptance of historical-critical methods had not yet become a test for liberalism or conservatism, much less for intellectual integrity itself.

All that was soon to change. Within a decade after Bushnell's death came the great surge of interest in the scientific study of the Bible that eventually brought critical studies to prominence in mainline Protestantism. It came swiftly, and not altogether peacefully. In 1876 Charles Augustus Briggs accepted appointment to the Davenport Chair of Hebrew and Cognate Languages at Union Theological Seminary. In 1879 William Rainey Harper began his career as teacher–scholar and academic entrepreneur at the Baptist Union Theological Seminary at Morgan Park. In 1880 Crawford Toy, whose views of the Bible came under attack at the Southern Baptist Theological Seminary in Louisville, Kentucky, took refuge at Harvard. In 1881 and 1886 the two installments of the revised version of the King James Bible appeared. By 1886 Andover Seminary had moved virtually en masse to a "progressive orthodoxy."

It was the liberals of the later nineteenth and the early twentieth century who saw to it that what William Beardslee aptly terms the "genetic paradigm"[3] would govern the work of any biblical scholar who laid claim to academic credibility. As before, but now in increased measure, the

---

[1] Arthur M. Schlesinger, Sr., "A Critical Period in American Religion," *Massachusetts Historical Society Proceedings* 64 (1930–32) 523–46; reprinted, Philadelphia: Fortress, 1967.

[2] Gladden, *Recollections*, 260; Roy Harrisville, *Benjamin Wisner Bacon: Pioneer in American Biblical Criticism* (Missoula, MT: Scholars Press/Society of Biblical Literature, 1976) 1 and n. 4.

[3] William Beardslee, *Literary Criticism of the New Testament.* Guides to Biblical Scholarship (Philadelphia: Fortress, 1970) 9–13.

works of the German masters became attractive to Americans who were eager to upgrade their standards of research. Inevitably, the choices confronting these scholars were projected back upon those facing their predecessors. Regardless of their denominational or doctrinal loyalties, Americans who had early on sought to "catch up" with European scholarship—Buckminster, Stuart, Parker, Edward Robinson, et al.— could be called "pioneers" of biblical criticism. Those who had ignored, missed, or opposed this development appeared fatally "uncritical" and "unscientific." Judged by this criterion, Bushnell would have to fall in the latter camp.

The conclusion that emerges from this study, however, is that his contribution to biblical studies was nonetheless real for being of a completely different order. In this regard the insightful observation of John Dillenberger and Claude Welch deserves special emphasis:

> We have spoken . . . of biblical criticism as posing certain problems for Christian thought. This does not mean, however, that the new conception of the Bible which came to characterize Protestant liberalism originated simply as a reaction to the discoveries of historical criticism. In fact, the situation was more nearly the reverse. It was new conceptions of religious authority and of the meaning of revelation which made possible the development of biblical criticism.[4]

It is precisely at this point that Bushnell was so significant.

His familiarity with the scholarship of Europe was not impressive. He was nevertheless knowledgeable enough, and independent enough, to attempt to reform the theological enterprise as a whole within a post-Kantian frame of reference.[5] By vesting religious authority somewhere other than in an infallibly inspired canon or an indisputable creed, by redefining the meaning of revelation, and by realigning relations among experience, text, and doctrine, he opened up new possibilities for the biblical scholars.

This by no means implies that he was the American "hero" who brought about this development. Such changes are not the work of an isolated individual, and in this case American interest in the mediating theologians of Germany and England was too widespread to justify such a claim. Yet the connection between theology and biblical studies in mid-nineteenth-century America was such that conditions were not all that favorable for the continuation of critical studies along the lines of Germany. The rational supernaturalists who were attracted to grammatical

---

4 Dillenberger and Welch, *Protestant Christianity*, 197.

5 On similarities between Bushnell and Ritschlianism, see George B. Stevens, "Horace Bushnell and Albrecht Ritschl: A Comparison," *Anglican Journal of Theology* 6 (1902) 35–36.

interpretation and even to textual criticism encountered not only Ernesti and Griesbach but also Semler, Lessing, Eichhorn, Schleiermacher, Baur, and—to their horror—Strauss. Even if so-called lower criticism seemed theologically productive, the results of so-called higher criticism could be accommodated in only piecemeal fashion. Thus lexicography, geography, antiquities, and textual variants might be studied, but when it came to no-holds-barred source criticism the risks outweighed the benefits. Only when evangelicals were given some assurance that this equation could be reversed could they embrace critical methods with enthusiasm, and that assurance was to come only when it was shown that words like orthodox and evangelical, and the values they represented, could gain a new lease on life if they were free of rational supernaturalist presuppositions about the essence of Christianity, the nature of religious language, and the validity of special revelation. Bushnell offered nothing less.

To later generations he did not offer much more. His proposals regarding the authority and the use of the Bible were compatible with the trajectory of thought from Schleiermacher to Ritschl, and in countless variations and with countless refinements they were incorporated into the theological methods of the new theologies. The proposal for a hermeneutics of aesthetic engagement, however, was not so well received. His "success" in interpreting the Bible in a way that "unlocked" and "revived" its meaning certainly made it possible for some to go and do likewise. Washington Gladden, for example, called the Preliminary Dissertation a "*Novum Organon,*" which gave him "a new sense of the nature of the instrument which I was trying to use, and making entirely clear the futility of the ordinary dogmatic method."[6] A "new world" was disclosed to him by the sermons of Bushnell and Robertson: "Here were men to whom spiritual truths were not traditions but living verities; men who knew how to bring religion into vital touch with reality."[7] Likewise, Henry Clay Trumbell had good words to say of Bushnell's work: "His service to me, as it has been to many another, was in bringing me to see that God's message or gift to us in the Scriptures is a gift to our 'imagination' rather than to our positive knowledge; that Bible truth, at the best, suggests to us far more than it can define."[8]

The careers of such "disciples," however, demonstrated that what they had learned from him was neither the *connection* between language and thought nor the *aesthetic* engagement with the Bible. They had learned, instead, that the Bible was not to be shackled by dogmatic literalism and that its "symbolic" passages, which accompanied and often

---

[6] Gladden, *Recollections*, 118–19.
[7] Ibid., 120.
[8] Trumbell, *My Four Teachers*, 10–11.

obscured its historical elements, could be translated into abiding truths about moral and spiritual values.

Indeed, when it came down to the specifics of his view of language and hermeneutics, Bushnell's grades plummeted. George Park Fisher gave Bushnell credit for exposing the folly of the Common Sense school when it attempted to *conceive* the objects of religious faith. Yet he concluded that Bushnell's theory of language was "crude" and "untenable."[9] Noah Porter remarked, somewhat ruefully, "it was unfortunate for his [Bushnell's] influence and reputation, that he was not better instructed and a more trustworthy interpreter of the New Testament scriptures."[10] Although "some of his interpretations" were truly "flashes of genius," Bushnell "was in no sense of the word a trustworthy exegete."[11] Frank Hugh Foster similarly claimed that Bushnell's theological correctives did not compensate for his inadequacy as a biblical scholar: "He never gives evidence of careful exegetical study of the Bible,—had, in fact, never had any competent training in its methods. He *saw*; but his vision was not always produced by the light that streams from the pages of the Bible."[12] Indeed, with the exception of Frank C. Porter, who sought to recognize the significance of the poetic character of the biblical texts,[13] liberal biblical scholars paid little heed to the Bushnellian statements about the way to relate symbol and thought, explication and application, or positivity and abiding truth.

It seems likely that Gladden and Trumbell, on the one hand, and Fisher, Noah Porter, and Foster, on the other, were correct. The retrospective glance at Bushnell's influence on liberalism made by W. H. Horton is especially pertinent: "The Essay on Language made it possible, in principle, to accept quite calmly all of the most radical results of Biblical criticism, since it made plain the distinction between the eternal idea of the Bible, which must always be grasped by intuition and experience, and its temporary thought form and modes of expression. . . ."[14] Bushnell's opposition to restrictive dogmatism was to help emancipate late nineteenth-century thinkers from bondage to orthodoxy, but his own biblical studies lacked the rigor, the precision, the breadth, and the depth to force the scholarly community into a methodology that was not *historical*-critical.

---

9 Fisher, "Horace Bushnell," 17–18.

10 Noah Porter, "Horace Bushnell: A Memorial Sermon preached in the Chapel of Yale College, Sunday, March 26th, 1876," *New Englander* 36 (1877) 160.

11 Ibid.

12 Foster, *Genetic History*, 406–11.

13 See Roy A. Harrisville, *Frank Chamberlain Porter: Pioneer in American Biblical Interpretation* (Missoula, MT: Scholars Press/Society of Biblical Literature, 1976), which deals with "the appreciative method" (pp. 13–20).

14 Horton, *Realistic Theology*, 30–31.

Sandwiched between Bushnell's uncritical acceptance of the historicity of most of the Bible and his penchant for didactic exposition was the notion that biblical language, like poetry, has a certain literary autonomy that provokes and shapes the answering imagination and therefore that the meaning of the text always emerges in the present. With historical-critical tools near at hand, liberals could not long tolerate his ambiguous treatment of history or of symbol. In the effort to clarify these matters, they were left with the distinction between the apparent and the "real" meaning of the text and sought to reconstruct the subject matter behind the text, whether it be "history" or "eternal truth." In so doing, they tended to lose sight of what lay at the heart of Bushnell's hermeneutical proposal. Means other than that of an imaginative engagement with biblical symbolism were employed in order to connect what the Bible "meant" with what it "means." Given the flaws in Bushnell's proposal, this outcome is quite understandable. Nonetheless, the decision to concentrate on the "genesis" of the texts rather than on their "forms" and "effects" has proved to be a fateful one for twentieth-century hermeneutics.

BIBLIOGRAPHY

This bibliography is divided into three sections. The first is a listing of Bushnell's publications, which reproduces, with additional detail, the bibliographical data compiled by Henry Barrett Learned (Horace Bushnell, *The Spirit in Man: Sermons and Selections*, Centenary Edition [New York: Charles Scribner's Sons, 1903] 445–73). The second section lists works of Bushnell's contemporaries that comment on his life and work. The third section notes sources written after 1876 that contain specific references to Bushnell. For newspaper articles appearing in *The Religious Herald*, obituaries and memorials in newspapers, and remarks on the dating of certain materials, the reader is directed to Learned's bibliography. No attempt has been made to trace the full publication history of Bushnell's works, and, given the currency of Bushnell's name, it is impossible to claim that an exhaustive inventory of secondary source materials has yet been made.

The library of Yale Divinity School is the repository of Bushnell's literary legacy, and a catalog of its holdings is available from that institution and is reprinted in the unpublished dissertation of Rachel Henderlite (see below). The National Union Catalog of Manuscript Collections identifies limited holdings elsewhere.

SECTION I

Bushnell's Published Works

1835

Sermon: "Crisis of the Church." Delivered at the North Church, Hartford, CT. Hartford: Daniel Burgess, 1835.

1837

Oration: "An Oration Pronounced Before the Society of Phi Beta Kappa, at New Haven, on the Principles of National Greatness, August 15, 1837." New Haven: Herrick and Noyes, 1837. Republished as "The True Wealth or Weal of Nations," in *Work and Play* (1864).

Article: "Spiritual Economy of Revivals of Religion." *Quarterly Christian Spectator* 10 (February 1838) 131–48. Republished in *Views of Christian Nurture* (1847) and in *Building Eras in Religion* (1881).

1839

Sermon: "A Discourse on the Slavery Question" [Acts 27:41]. Delivered in the North

Church, Hartford, Thursday Evening, 10 January 1839. Hartford: Case, Tiffany, 1839. Pp. 32.

Address: "Revelation." Delivered before the Porter Rhetorical Society at Andover, MA, on Tuesday afternoon, 13 September 1839. For contemporary comment see *Boston Recorder*, 13 September 1839. Excerpts are published in *The Spirit in Man* (1903); a transcription is available in David Stanley Steward, "Horace Bushnell and Contemporary Christian Education" (Ph.D. diss., Yale University, 1966) 308–35.

1840

Sermon: "American Politics" [John 19:21]. *American National Preacher* 14 (December 1840) 189–204.

1842

Address: "The Stability of Change." Delivered at the Commencement of Western Reserve College, Hudson, Ohio, 9 August 1842. This address was probably substantially the same as that published as "Of the Mutabilities of Life," in *Moral Uses of Dark Things* (1868). For contemporary comment, see *Ohio Observer*, 18 August 1842.

Lecture: "The Vital Principle." Delivered at Western Reserve College, Hudson, Ohio, 9 August 1842. Published as "Life, or the Lives," in *Work and Play* (1864).

1843

Article: "Taste and Fashion," *New Englander* 1 (April 1843)) 153–68.

Oration: "A Discourse on the Moral Tendencies and Results of Human History." Delivered before the Society of Alumni in Yale College, on Wednesday, 16 August 1843. New Haven: T. H. Pease, 1843. Pp. 39. Republished as "The Growth of Law," in *Work and Play* (1864).

Letter: "To the Editor of *The Religious Herald*." Dated 14 December 1843. *The Religious Herald* (Hartford), 20 December 1843.

1844

Article: "Review of the Errors of the Times." *New Englander* 2 (January 1844) 143–75. Reprinted, with a prefatory note, as *Review of the Errors of the Times, a Charge, by the Rt. Rev. T. C. Brownell, D.D., LL.D., Bishop of the Diocese of Connecticut.* Hartford: E. Hunt, 1844. Pp. 51.

Sermon: "The Great Time Keeper" [Gen 1:14]. *American National Preacher* 18 (January 1844) 1–9.

Letter: "To *The Religious Herald*" (Hartford), 24 January 1844.

Letter: "A Church Without a Bishop." *The Religious Herald* (Hartford), 20 March 1844.

Sermon: "Politics under the Law of God" [Isa 30:11]. A Discourse delivered in the North Congregational Church, Hartford, on the Annual Fast of 1844. Hartford: E. Hunt, 1844. Pp. 23.

Article: "The Kingdom of Heaven as a Grain of Mustard Seed." *New Englander* 2 (October 1844) 600–619. Republished as "Growth, Not Conquest, the True Method of Christian Progress," in *Views of Christian Nurture* (1847).

Letter: "Reply to Dr. Taylor." Signed "Constans." *Christian Freeman* (Hartford), 12 December 1844.

1845

Sermon: "Discourse on the Moral Uses of the Sea" [Gen 1:10]. Delivered on board the packet-ship *Victoria*, Captain Morgan, at sea, July 1845. New York:

M. W. Dodd, 1845. Pp. 20. Revised for publication as "Of the Sea," in *Moral Uses of Dark Things* (1880).

Letter: "A Letter from Dr. Bushnell." Dated Geneva, 7 October 1845. *The Religious Herald* (Hartford), 8 November 1845.

1846

Letter: ["The Oregon Question"]. Addressed to the Editor of the *London Universe*, 3 March 1846. Signed "An American." Reprinted as "Dr. Bushnell in London," *The Religious Herald* (Hartford), 4 April 1846.

Letter: "A Letter to His Holiness, Pope Gregory XVI." Dated London, 2 April 1846. London: Ward and Co., 1846. Reprinted as "Letter to the Pope among the Papists," *The Religious Herald* (Hartford), 9 May 1846, and in *Building Eras in Religion* (1881).

Sermon: "Unconscious Influence" [John 20:8]. London, 1846. Republished as "Influence of Example," in *American National Preacher* 20 (August 1846), and in *Sermons for the New Life* (1858).

Sermon: "Uses and Duties of Stormy Sundays" [Ps 118:8]. *American Pulpit* 2 (October 1846) 123–33.

Address: "An Address Before the Hartford County Agricultural Society." Delivered 2 October 1846. Hartford: Brown and Parsons, 1846. Pp. 24. Republished as "Agriculture at the East," in *Work and Play* (editions from 1864 to 1881).

Sermon: "The Day of Roads" [Judg 5:6]. A Discourse delivered on the Annual Thanksgiving, 1846. Hartford: Elihu Greer, 1846. Pp. 35. Republished in *Work and Play* (1864).

1847

Article: "The Evangelical Alliance." *New Englander* 5 (January 1847) 102–25. Reprint. New York: Baker and Scribner, Brick Church Chapel, 1847. Pp. 32.

Letter: "Addressed to the North Consociation of Hartford County." *New England Religious Herald* (Hartford), 9 January 1847.

Sermon: "Prosperity our Duty" [2 Chr 32:20]. A Discourse delivered at the North Church, Hartford, Sabbath evening, 31 January 1847. Hartford: Case, Tiffany and Burnham, 1847. Pp. 24. Republished in *The Spirit in Man* (1903).

Book: *Discourses on Christian Nurture.* Approved by the Committee of Publication. Boston: Massachusetts Sabbath School Society, 1847. Pp. 72. [Introductory note and two discourses].

Letter: "To the Editor of *The New England Religious Herald.*" *New England Religious Herald* (Hartford), 16 October 1847.

Pamphlet: *An Argument for "Discourses on Christian Nurture."* Addressed to the Publishing Committee of the Massachusetts Sabbath School Society. Hartford: E. Hunt, 1847. Republished in *Views of Christian Nurture* (1847).

Address: "Barbarism the First Danger" [Judg 27:13]. A Discourse for Home Missions. New York: The American Home Missionary Society, 1847. Pp. 32. Republished in *Work and Play* (2d ed.).

Book: *Views of Christian Nurture, and of Subjects Adjacent Thereto.* Hartford: E. Hunt, 1847; 2d ed., 1848. Reprint. Delmar, New York: School Facsimiles and Reprints, 1975. Contents: Discourse (I) on Christian Nurture. Discourse (II) on Christian Nurture. Argument for Discourses on Christian Nurture. Spiritual Economy of Revivals of Religion (see 1838). Growth, Not Conquest, the True Method of Christian Progress (see 1844). The Organic Unity of the Family (a sermon, Jer 7:18). The Scene of the Pentecost and a Christian Parish (a sermon, Acts 2:44–47).

1848

Article: "Christian Comprehensiveness." *New Englander* 6 (January 1848) 81–111. Republished in *Building Eras in Religion* (1881).

Address: "A Discourse on the Atonement." Delivered before the Divinity School in Harvard University, 9 July 1848. Published in *God in Christ* (1849).

Addresss: "Concio Ad Clerum: A Discourse on the Divinity of Christ." Delivered at the Annual Commencement of Yale College, 15 August 1848. Published in *God in Christ* (1849).

Oration: "Work and Play." An Oration delivered before the Society of Phi Beta Kappa, at Cambridge, 24 August 1848. Cambridge: G. Nichols, 1848. Pp. 39. Republished in *Work and Play* (1864).

Address: "A Discourse on Dogma and Spirit; or the True Reviving of Religion." Delivered before the Porter Rhetorical Society, at Andover, September 1848. Published in *God in Christ* (1849).

1849

Book: *God in Christ, Three Discourses delivered at New Haven, Cambridge, and Andover, with a Preliminary Dissertation on Language.* Hartford: Brown and Parsons, 1849. Pp. 356. Reprint. New York: AMS Press, n.d.

Sermon: "The Moral Uses of Great Pestilences" [Deut 29:24]. A Discourse delivered in the North Church, Hartford, on the Occasion of the National Fast, 3 August 1849. *American Literary Magazine* 5 (August 1849) 81–94. Reprint. Hartford: J. Gaylord Wells, 1849. Republished as "Of Plague and Pestilence," in *Moral Uses of Dark Things* (1868).

1850

Oration: "The Fathers of New England." Delivered before the New England Society of New York, 21 December 1849. New York: George P. Putnam, 1850. Pp. 44. Republished as "The Founders Great in their Unconsciousness," in *Work and Play* (1864).

1851

Book: *Christ in Theology: Being the Answer of the Author before the Hartford Central Association of Ministers, October, 1849, for the Doctrines of the Book entitled "God in Christ."* Hartford: Brown and Parsons, 1851. Pp. 348.

Address: "Speech for Connecticut." Being an Historical Estimate of the State, delivered before the Legislature and other invited guests at the Festival of the Normal School in New Britain, June 4, 1851. Hartford: Boswell and Saxon, 1851. Pp. 43. Republished as "Historical Estimate of Connecticut," in *Work and Play* (1864).

Discourse: "The Age of Homespun." Delivered at Litchfield, CT, on the occasion of the Centennial Celebration, 1851. In *Litchfield County Centennial Celebration.* Hartford: E. Hunt, 1851. Pp. 107–30. Republished in *Work and Play* (1864).

1852

Discourse: "Religious Music" [1 Cor 14:7]. Hartford: F. A. Brown, 1852. Pp. 26. Republished in *Work and Play* (1864).

Lecture: ["Revealed Religion"] [Rom 8:22]. Cambridge, MA, Harvard College Library. Published as chap. 15, *Nature and the Supernatural* (1858).

Letter: "Remonstrance from Dr. Bushnell." Addressed to the General Association of Connecticut. *New England Religious Herald* (Hartford), 19 June 1852.

1853

Sermon: "Common Schools" [Lev 24:22]. A Discourse on the Modifications demanded by the Roman Catholics, delivered in the North Church, Hartford, on the day of the late Fast, 25 March 1853. Hartford: n.p., 1853. Pp. 24. Republished in *Building Eras in Religion* (1881).

Sermon: "Twentieth Anniversary" [Phil 1:4]. A Commemorative Discourse delivered in the North Church, Hartford, 22 May 1853. Hartford: E. Geer, 1853. Pp. 32.

Report: *Report of the Committee concerning the Proposed Public Park.* To the Honorable, the Court of Common Council of the City of Hartford, 14 November 1853. Pp. 8. [The substance of the report was Bushnell's.]

1854

Sermon: "The Northern Iron" [Jer 15:12]. A Discourse delivered in the North Church, Hartford, on the Annual State Fast, 14 April 1854. Hartford: E. Hunt and Son, 1854. Pp. 29.

Letter: "Addressed to Rev. Dr. Hawes." Dated Hartford, 3 April 1854. *New England Religious Herald* (Hartford), 1 June 1854. See Mary Bushnell Cheyney, *Life and Letters*, 337.

Speech: By Dr. Bushnell at the General Association of Connecticut (New Haven), in June 1854. Excerpts in *New England Religious Herald* (Hartford), 6 July 1854.

Article: "The Christian Trinity, a Practical Truth." *New Englander* 12 (November 1854) 485–509. Republished in *Building Eras in Religion* (1881).

1855

Letter: "Correspondence." Dated New York, 15 January 1855. *New England Religious Herald* (Hartford), 18 January 1855.

Letter: "Letter from Dr. Bushnell." Dated San Francisco, 19 May 1856. *Independent* (New York), 3 July 1856.

Sermon: "Society and Religion" [Jer 1:10]. A Sermon for California delivered on Sabbath evening, 6 July 1856, at the installation of Rev. E. S. Lacy as Pastor of the First Congregational Church, San Francisco. Hartford: L. E. Hunt, 1856. Pp. 32.

1857

Appeal: *Movement for a University in California: A Statement to the Public by the Trustees of the College of California, and an Appeal by Dr. Bushnell.* San Francisco: Pacific Publishing Company, 1857. Pp. 15.

Sermon: "Spiritual Dislodgements [Jer 48:11]. A Sermon of Reunion, preached in the North Church, Hartford, 22 February 1857. Hartford: L. E. Hunt, 1857. Pp. 21. Republished in *Sermons for the New Life* (1858).

Sermon: "A Week-Day Sermon to the Business Men of Hartford" [Acts 27:15]. Supplement to *The Courant* (Hartford), 31 October 1857. Republished in *The Spirit in Man* (1903).

Sermon: "Thanksgiving for Kansas" [Num 11:10]. Delivered on 26 November 1857, in Hartford. See Mary Bushnell Cheyney, *Life and Letters*, 411. [Published in whole or in part in an unidentified newspaper.]

1858

Article: "California, Its Characteristics and Prospects." *New Englander* 16 (February 1858) 142–82. Reprint. San Francisco: Whitton, Towne, and Co., 1858. Pp. 32.

Address: "City Plans." Written for the Public Improvement Society of Hartford. Date uncertain. Published in *Work and Play* (1864).

Book: *Sermons for the New Life.* New York: Charles Scribner, 1858. Pp. 456. Revised in 1903. Contents: (I) Every Man's Life a Plan of God; (II) The Spirit in Man; (III) Dignity of Human Nature Shown from its Ruins; (IV) The Hunger of the Soul; (V) The Reason of Faith; (VI) Regeneration; (VII) The Personal Love and Lead of Christ; (VIII) Light on the Cloud; (IX) Capacity of Religion Extirpated by Disuse; (X) Unconscious Influence; (XI) Obligation a Privilege; (XII) Happiness and Joy; (XIII) True Problem of Christian Experience; (XIV) Lost Purity Restored; (XV) Living to God in Small Things; (XVI) Power of an Endless Life; (XVII) Respectable Sin; (XVIII) Power of God in Self-Sacrifice; (XIX) Duty Not Measured by Our Own Ability; (XX) He That Knows God Will Confess Him; (XXI) Efficiency of the Passive Virtues; (XXII) Spiritual Dislodgement; (XXIII) Christ as Separate from the World.

Book: *Nature and the Supernatural, as together constituting the One System of God.* New York: Charles Scribner, 1858. Pp. 528. Reprint. New York: AMS Press, n.d.

Tract: *Position and Power.* Occasional, No. 2. Boston: American Tract Society, 1858. Pp. 8.

Letter: "Correspondence." Letter in reply to one from the North Church and Society [17 May 1858]. Dated Hartford, 15 June 1858; addressed to Normand Smith, A. M. Collins, and others. *New England Religious Herald* (Hartford). 8 July 1858.

1859

Sermon: "Parting Words" [Jer 27:10]. A Discourse delivered in the North Church, Hartford, 3 July 1859. Hartford: L. E. Hunt, 1859. Pp. 25.

Letter: "To *The Courant*, Hartford." Dated St. Anthony, MN, August 1859. In *The Courant* (Hartford), 12 August 1859.

1860

Sermon: "The Census and Slavery" [Isa 26:15]. A Thanksgiving Discourse delivered in the Chapel at Clifton Springs, NY, 29 November 1860. Hartford: L. E. Hunt. 1860. Pp. 24.

1861

Book: *The Character of Jesus: Forbidding His Possible Classification with Men.* New York: Charles Scribner, 1861 (c. 1860). Reprint, with slight revisions, *Nature and the Supernatural*, chap. 10. Pp. 173.

Book: *Christian Nurture* [Isa 54:13]. New York: Charles Scribner, 1861 (c. 1860). Pp. 407. Reprint. Grand Rapids: Baker Books, 1979. Contents: Part I: The Doctrine. (I) What Christian Nurture Is; (II) What Christian Nurture Is; (III) Ostrich Nurture; (IV) Organic Unity of the Family; (V) Apostolic Authority, How Developed; (VI) Apostolic Authority of Infant Baptism; (VII) Church Membership of Children; (VIII) Out-Populating Power of the Christian Stock. Part II: The Mode. (I) When and Where Nurture Begins; (II) Parental Qualifications; (III) Physical Nurture to be a Means of Grace; (IV) Treatment that Discourages Piety; (V) Family Government; (VI) Plays and Pastimes, Holidays and Sundays; (VII) Christian Teaching of Children; (VIII) Family Prayers.

Sermon: "Reverses Needed" [Prov 24:10]. A Discourse delivered on the Sunday (28 July 1861) after the Disaster of Bull Run, in the North Church, Hartford. Hartford: L. E. Hunt, 1861. Pp. 27. Republished in *The Spirit in Man* (1903).

1863

Article: "The Doctrine of Loyalty." *New Englander* 22 (July 1863) 560-81. Republished in *Work and Play* (1864).

1864

Book: *Work and Play; or Literary Varieties.* New York: Charles Scribner, 1864. Pp. 464. Rev. eds. in 1881 and 1903. Contents: (I) Work and Play; (II) True Wealth or Weal of Nations; (III) Growth of Law; (IV) Founders Great in Their Unconsciousness; (V) Historical Estimate of Connecticut; (VI) Agriculture at the East; (VII) Life, or the Lives; (VIII) City Plans; (IX) Doctrine of Loyalty; (X) Age of Homespun; (XI) Day of Roads; (XII) Religious Music. [Revisions of 1881 and thereafter substitute "Barbarism the First Danger" for "Agriculture at the East."]

Book: *Christ and His Salvation: In Sermons Variously Related Thereto.* New York: Charles Scribner, 1864. Pp. 456. [Rev. ed., 1877: *Sermons on Christ and His Salvation.*] Contents: (I) Christ Waiting To Find Room; (II) The Gentleness of God; (III) The Insight of Love; (IV) Salvation for the Lost Condition; (V) The Fasting and Temptation of Jesus; (VI) Conviction of Sin by the Cross; (VII) Christ Asleep; (VIII) Christian Ability; (IX) Integrity and Grace; (X) Liberty and Discipline; (XI) Christ's Agony, or Moral Suffering; (XII) The Physical Suffering, or Cross of Christ; (XIII) Salvation by Man; (XIV) The Bad Consciousness Taken Away; (XV) The Bad Mind Makes a Bad Element; (XVI) Present Relations of Christ with His Followers; (XVII) The Wrath of the Lamb; (XVIII) Christian Forgiveness; (XIX) Christ Bearing the Sins of Transgressors; (XX) The Putting on of Christ; (XXI) Heaven Opened.

Sermon: "Popular Government by Divine Right" [Jer 30:21]. Delivered on the Late National Thanksgiving (24 November 1864), in the South Church, Hartford, before the congregations of that and the South Baptist Church. Hartford: L. E. Hunt, 1864. Pp. 16. Republished in *Building Eras in Religion.* (1881).

1865

Article: "Abjuration of America." *Hours at Home* 1 (July 1865) 244–45.

Oration: "Our Obligations to the Dead." Delivered at the Commemorative Celebration, held 26 July 1865, in honor of the Alumni of Yale College who were in the Military or Naval Service of the United States during the Recent War. In *Yale College Alumni: Addresses and Proceedings of the Commemorative Celebration.* New Haven: n.p., 1866. Pp. 9–38. Republished in *Building Eras in Religion* (1881).

1866

Book: *The Vicarious Sacrifice, Grounded in Principles of Universal Obligation.* New York: Charles Scribner, 1866 (c. 1865). Pp. 552. (See 1874 and 1877).

Article: "The Natural History of the Yaguey Family." *Hours at Home* 2 (March 1866) 413–18.

Sermon: "Religious Nature and Religious Character" [Acts 17:27]. *Monthly Religious Magazine* 35 (March 1866) 156–69.

Address: "Pulpit Talent." Delivered before the Porter Rhetorical Society of Andover Theological Seminary at the Anniversary, September 1866. *Hours at Home* 3 (October 1866) 485–99. Republished in *Building Eras in Religion* (1881).

Sermon: ["Discourse in Memory of Rev. Dr. Noah Porter"] [Ps 71:9]. In *Memorial of Noah Porter, D.D., late of Farmington, Connecticut, comprising the Discourses of President T. D. Woolsey, Rev. L. Paine, and Horace Bushnell, D.D., occasioned by his death*. Farmington: S. S. Cowles, 1867. Pp. 41–63.

Article: "How to Make a Ripe and Right Old Age." *Hours at Home* 4 (December 1866) 106–12.

1867

Article: "Moral Uses of Dark Things. I. Of Night and Sleep." *Hours at Home* 4 (February 1867) 289–97. Republished in *Moral Uses of Dark Things* (1868).

Article: "II. Of Non-Intercourse between Worlds." *Hours at Home* 4 (March 1867) 385–93. Republished in *Moral Uses of Dark Things* (1868).

Sermon: "Building Eras in Religion." Delivered at the Dedication of the Park Church, Hartford, CT, on Friday evening, 29 March 1867. *Hours at Home* 7 (September 1868) 385–94. Republished in *Building Eras in Religion* (1881).

Article: "III. Of Bad Government or Bad Men in Power." *Hours at Home* 4 (April 1867) 481–88. Republished in *Moral Uses of Dark Things* (1868).

Article: "IV. Of Want and Waste." *Hours at Home* 5 (May 1867) 1–9. Republished in *Moral Uses of Dark Things* (1868).

Article. "V. Of the Conditions of Solidarity." *Hours at Home* 5 (June 1867) 97–105. Republished in *Moral Uses of Dark Things* (1868).

Article: "VI. Of Oblivion or Dead History." *Hours at Home* 5 (July 1867) 212–20. Republished in *Moral Uses of Dark Things* (1868).

Article: "VII. Of the Animal Infestations." *Hours at Home* 5 (August 1867) 307–15. Republished in *Moral Uses of Dark Things* (1868).

Article: "VIII. Of Physical Pain." *Hours at Home* 5 (September 1867) 385–94. Republished in *Moral Uses of Dark Things* (1868).

Sermon: "The Value One Man Has to Another" [2 Cor 12:14]. *Advance* (Chicago), 5 September 1867. Republished as "The Property Right We Are to Get in Souls," in *Sermons on Living Subjects* (1872).

Article: "IX. Of Things Unsightly and Disgustful." *Hours at Home* 6 (November 1867) 1–9. Republished in *Moral Uses of Dark Things* (1868).

Article: "X. Of Insanity." *Hours at Home* 6 (December 1867) 97–106. Republished in *Moral Uses of Dark Things* (1868).

1868

Article: "XI. Of Physical Danger." *Hours at Home* 6 (January 1868) 193–201. Republished in *Moral Uses of Dark Things* (1868).

Sermon: "What It Is to Preach Christ" [2 Cor 4:6]. *Advance* (Chicago), 2 January 1868. Republished as "The Gospel of the Face," in *Sermons on Living Subjects* (1872).

Article: "XII. Of the Mutabilities of Life." *Hours at Home* 6 (February 1868) 296–305. Republished in *Moral Uses of Dark Things* (1868).

Article: "The Law of Feeding as Pertaining to Souls." *Advance* (Chicago), 13 February 1868.

Article: "The Learning How to Feed." *Advance* (Chicago), 13 February 1868.

Article: "XIII. Of Winter." *Hours at Home* 6 (March 1868) 406–14. Republished in *Moral Uses of Dark Things* (1868).

Article: "Science and Religion." *Putnam's Magazine* 1 (March 1868) 25–75.

Article: "Meaning and Use of the Lord's Supper." *Advance* (Chicago), 5 March 1868.

Address: "Training for the Pulpit Manward." Delivered at the decennial anniversary of the Chicago Theological Seminary, before the Rhetorical Society, Wednesday, 29 April 1868. *Hours at Home* 7 (July 1868) 193–203. Republished in *Building Eras in Religion* (1881).

Article: "Distinctions of Color," *Hours at Home* 7 (May 1868) 81–89. Republished in *Moral Uses of Dark Things* (1868).

Book: *Moral Uses of Dark Things.* New York: Charles Scribner, 1868. Pp. 360. Rev. eds. in 1881 and 1903. Contents: (I) Of Night and Sleep; (II) Of Want and Waste; (III) Of Bad Government; (IV) Of Oblivion, or Dead History; (V) Of Physical Pain; (VI) Of Physical Danger; (VII) Of the Conditions of Solidarity; (VIII) Of Non-Intercourse between Worlds; (IX) Of Winter; (X) Of Things Unsightly and Disgustful; (XI) Of Plague and Pestilence; (XII) Of Insanity; (XIII) Of the Animal Infestation; (XIV) Of Distinctions of Color; (XV) Of the Mutabilities of Life; (XVI) Of the Sea.

1869

Article: "Progress." *Hours at Home* 8 (January 1869) 199–210.

Article: "Hartford Park." *Hearth and Home* 1 (6 February 1869) 101–2. Reprinted almost in its entirety in Cheyney, *Life and Letters*, 312–19.

Sermon: "God's Thoughts Fit Bread for Children" [Ps 134:17]. A Sermon preached before the Connecticut Sunday-School Teachers' Convention at the Pearl Street Congregational Church, Hartford, CT, Tuesday evening, 2 March 1869. Boston: Nichols and Noyes, 1869. Pp. 38. Republished in *The Spirit in Man* (1903).

Book: *Women's Suffrage: The Reform Against Nature.* New York: Charles Scribner, 1869. Pp. 184. Reprint. Washington, DC: Zenger, 1976.

Article: "Our Gospel, A Gift to the Imagination." *Hours at Home* 10 (December 1869) 159–72. Republished in *Building Eras in Religion* (1881).

1870

Address: "The New Education. Delivered at the Annual Commencement of the Sheffield Scientific School, New Haven, 18 July 1870." *Hours at Home* 11 (September 1870) 421–34. Republished in *Building Eras in Religion* (1881).

1871

Articles: "A Series on the Subject of Prayer," printed in *Advance* (Chicago), 4 (1871–72). (I) "Prayer accorded as a Right of Petition" (13 April 1871); (II) "Ends for which Prayer is Instituted" (27 April 1871); (III) "By What in a Prayer Does It Prevail?" (18 May 1871); (IV) "Prayer as Related to Second Causes" (8 June 1871); (V) "Prayer as Related to God's Will" (29 June 1871); (VI) "Prayer in the Name of Christ" (13 July 1871); (VII) "The Prayer of Faith" (3 August 1871); (VIII) "Induement with Character through Prayer" (31 August 1871); (IX) "The Testing of Prayer" (3 October 1872).

Letter: "The Conflagration." Letter from Dr. Bushnell, dated Hartford, November 1871. *Advance* (Chicago), 16 November 1871.

Letter: "To Henry W. Longfellow." Dated Hartford, 28 December 1871. In *Final Memorials of Henry Wadsworth Longfellow*, by Samuel Longfellow, Boston: Ticknor, 1887. Pp. 178–79. Printed also in *Longfellow's Life*, rev. ed., 3:192–93; and in *Henry Wadsworth Longfellow*, by T. W. Higginson. Boston and New York: Houghton, Mifflin, 1902. Pp. 245–46.

1872

Speech: "The Capitol Site." *The Courant* (Hartford), 8 January 1872.

Book: *Sermons on Living Subjects*. New York: Scribner, Armstrong and Co., 1872. Pp. 468. Contents: (I) Mary, The Mother of Jesus; (II) Loving God is but Letting God Love Us; (III) Feet and Wings; (IV) Gospel of the Face; (V) The Completing of the Soul; (VI) The Immediate Knowledge of God; (VII) Religious Nature and Religious Character; (VIII) The Property Right We Are To Get in Souls; (IX) The Dissolving of Doubts; (X) Christ Regenerates Even the Desires; (XI) A Single Trial Better Than Many; (XII) Self-examination Examined; (XIII) How to be a Christian in Trade; (XIV) In and by Things Temporal are Given Things Eternal; (XV) God Organizing in the Church; (XVI) Routine Observance Indispensable; (XVII) Our Advantage in being Finite; (XVIII) The Outside Saints; (XIX) Free to Amusements, and Too Free to Want Them; (XX) The Military Discipline; (XXI) The Coronation of the Lamb; (XXII) Our Relations to Christ in the Future Life.

1874

Book: *Forgiveness and Law, Grounded in Principles Interpreted by Human Analogies*. New York: Scribner, Armstrong, 1874. Pp. 256. See *The Vicarious Sacrifice* (1877).

1875

Paper: "Inspiration by the Holy Spirit." In *The Spirit in Man* (1903).

1877

Book: *The Vicarious Sacrifice: Grounded in Principles Interpreted by Human Analogies*. New York: Charles Scribner, 1877. 2 vols. Vol. 1, pp. 552; Vol. 2, pp. 269. For this edition, *Forgiveness and Law* (1874) is revised by the addition of previously unpublished notes (pp. 259–69) and included as vol. 2.

1881

Book: *Building Eras in Religion*. Literary Varieties, III. New York: Charles Scribner's Sons, 1881. Pp. 459. Contents: (I) Building Eras in Religion; (II) The New Education; (III) Common Schools; (IV) The Christian Trinity a Practical Truth; (V) Spiritual Economy of Revivals of Religion; (VI) Pulpit Talent; (VII) Training for the Pulpit Manward; (VIII) Our Gospel a Gift to the Imagination; (IX) Popular Government by Divine Right; (X) Our Obligations to the Dead; (XI) Letter to his Holiness, Pope Gregory XVI; (XII) Christian Comprehensiveness.

1903

Book: *The Spirit in Man: Sermons and Selections*. New York: Charles Scribner's Sons, 1903. Pp. 473. Contents: Part I. Inspiration by the Holy Spirit. Part II. Sermons (eleven). Part III. Selections from Sermons (twenty-seven). Part IV. Ceremony of Marriage; A Group of Letters; Aphorisms; Bibliography.

SECTION 2

Contemporary Works

1838

"[Notice of] An Oration by Mr. Horace Bushnell pronounced before the Society of Phi Beta Kappa at New Haven, August 15, 1837." *North American Review* 46 (January 1838) 301–2.

1839

Gillette, Francis. *A Review of the Rev. Horace Bushnell's "Discourse on the Slavery Question," delivered in the North Church, Hartford, January 10, 1839.* Hartford: S. S. Cowles, 1839.

1843

Catholicus [pseud.]. *A Letter to Dr. Bushnell, of Hartford, on the Rationalistic, Socinian, and Infidel Tendency of Certain Passages in his Address before the Alumni of Yale College.* Hartford: H. S. Parsons, 1843.

"[Review of] 'A Discourse before the Alumni of Yale College, August 16, 1843,' by Horace Bushnell." *New Englander* 1 (October 1843) 597–600.

1846

"[Review of] 'Unconscious Influence: A Sermon,' by Reverend Horace Bushnell." *New Englander* 4 (July 1846) 451–52.

1847

"Alleged Suppression of Dr. Bushnell's Book." *Boston Recorder* 32 (7 October 1847) 158.

B., G. W. "Bushnell on Christian Nurture." *Christian Examiner and Religious Miscellany* 43, 4th s. 8 (November 1847) 435–51.

"Dr. Tyler's Letter to Dr. Bushnell on Christian Nurture." *New England Puritan* 1 (1847) 323–30.

[Hodge, Charles.] "Bushnell on Christian Nurture." *Biblical Repertory and Princeton Review*, n.s. 19 (October 1847) 502–39. Reprint. *Essays and Reviews: Selected from the Princeton Review.* New York: Robert Carter and Brothers, 1857 (c. 1856).

Nevin, John Williamson. "Educational Religion." *Weekly Messenger of the German Reformed Church*, n.s. 12 (23, 30 June and 7, 14 July 1847). See also comments in 11, 25 August and 1 September 1847.

[Porter, Noah.] "New Theological Controversy." *New Englander* 5 (October 1847) 613–14.

"Review of Horace Bushnell's *Discourses on Christian Nurture.*" *Christian Observatory* 1 (July 1847) 323–30.

Tyler, Bennett. *A Letter to Rev. Bushnell which discusses his book "Discourses on Christian Nurture."* Dated East Windsor Hill, 7 June 1847. Printed as pamphlet. N.p.: Massachusetts Sabbath School Society, 1847.

1848

"Bushnell's Christian Nurture." *Church Review and Ecclesiastical Register* 1 (July 1848) 228–45.

Porter, Noah. "Bushnell on Christian Nurture." *New Englander* 6 (January 1848) 120–47.

"[Review of] 'An Oration delivered before the Society of Phi Beta Kappa . . . ,' by Horace Bushnell." *New Englander* 6 (October 1848) 597–98.

Tyler, Bennett. *Letters to the Rev. Dr. Horace Bushnell, D.D., on Christian Nurture, containing strictures on his book, entitled "Views of Christian Nurture, and Subjects Adjacent Thereto."* Hartford: Brown and Parsons, 1848.

1849

[Bacon, Leonard.] "[Review of] *God in Christ* . . . , by Horace Bushnell; '*Review of Dr. Bushnell's Theories of Incarnation and Atonement* . . . ,' by Robert

Turnbull; 'What Does Dr. Bushnell Mean? From the *New York Evangelist.*' *New Englander* 7, n.s. 1 (May 1849) 324–26.

Brownson, Orestes Augustus. "Bushnell's Discourses [Review of *God in Christ*]." In *Works of Orestes A. Brownson*, 7:1–116. Compiled by Henry F. Brownson. Detroit: T. Nourse, 1882–1907. Reprint. New York: AMS Press, 1966. [Reprinted from *Brownson's Quarterly Review* 3–4 (1849–51]).

"Bushnell's Book [*God in Christ*]." *Boston Recorder* 24 (23 March, 30 March, 6 April, 11 May 1849) 46, 50, 54, 74.

"[Review of] Bushnell's *God in Christ*." *Biblical Repository and Classical Review*, 3rd s. 5 (April 1849) 371–72.

[Chesebrough, Amos Sheffield.] *Contributions of CC: Now Declared in full as Criticus Criticorum.* Hartford: Brown and Parsons, 1849. [Ten articles, six of which appeared in *New England Religious Herald*, 7, 14, 21, 28 July and 4, 18 August.

Goodwin, Henry M. "Thoughts, Words and Things." *Bibliotheca Sacra* 6 (May 1849) 271–300.

[Hodge, Charles.] "Bushnell's Discourses: Review of *God in Christ*, by Horace Bushnell." *Biblical Repertory and Princeton Review*, n.s. 21 (April 1849) 259–98.

[Morison, J. H.] "Bushnell's Discourses [*God in Christ*]." *Christian Examiner and Religious Miscellany* 46, 4th s. 11 (September 1849) 453–84.

_____ . "Replies to Horace Bushnell." *Christian Examiner and Religious Miscellany* 47, 4th s. 12 (December 1849) 238–47.

Lord, David N. "Dr. Bushnell's 'Dissertation on Language.'" *Theological and Literary Journal* 2 (July 1849) 61–130.

_____ ."Dr. Bushnell's Discourses [*God in Christ*]." *Theological and Literary Journal* 2 (October 1849) 173–222.

Omicron. [Goodrich, Chauncey A.] *What Does Dr. Bushnell Mean? From "The New York Evangelist, 1848."* Hartford: Case, Tiffany, 1849.

Pond, Enoch, *Review of Dr. Bushnell's "God in Christ."* Bangor: E. F. Duren, 1849.

"Review of *God in Christ*." *Christian Observatory* 3 (June 1849) 329–30.

"Review of *God in Christ*, by Horace Bushnell." *Methodist Quarterly Review*, 4th s. 1 (April 1849) 329–30.

Smith, Henry Boynton. "The Relations of Faith and Philosophy." *Bibliotheca Sacra* 6 (November 1849) 673–709. Reprint. *Faith and Philosophy: Discourses and Essays by Henry B. Smith.* Edited by George L. Prentiss. New York: Scribner, Armstrong, 1877.

Turnbull, Robert. *Review of Dr. Bushnell's Theories of the Incarnation and Atonement (A Supplement to "Theophany").* College Pamphlets, vol. 671. Hartford: n.p., 1849.

1850

Haven, Joseph. "The Doctrine of the Trinity: Review of *God in Christ*, by Horace Bushnell." *New Englander* 8 (February 1850) 1–29.

Minutes of the General Association of Connecticut at their Meeting in Litchfield. New Haven: n.p., 1850.

Park, Edwards Amasa. "Theology of the Intellect and That of the Feelings." *Bibliotheca Sacra* 7 (July 1850) 553–69. Reprint. *American Philosophic Addresses*, edited by Joseph L. Blau. Pp. 627–58.

"Position of Congregationalism. Report of the Committee of the Central Association of Hartford County, on Dr. Bushnell's book entitled, *God in Christ*," *Church Review and Ecclesiastical Register* 2 (January 1850) 559–73.

Remonstrance and Complaint of the Association of Fairfield West to the Hartford Central Association. Together with the Reply of the Hartford Central Association. New York: Benedict, 1850.

"Taylorism-Bushnellism and Parkerism." *Independent* 2 (11 July 1850) 114.

1851

Ellis, G. E. "[Review of] *Christ in Theology*." *Christian Examiner and Religious Miscellany* 50, 4th s. 15 (May 1851) 513–14.

Hayden, William B. "Professor Park's Discourse." *New Jerusalem Magazine* 24 (January 1851) 10–21.

Kilbourne, Payne Kenyon. *A Biographical History of Litchfield County, Connecticut.* New York: Clark, Austin, 1851.

"Review of *Christ in Theology* by Horace Bushnell." *New Englander* 9 (May 1851) 310–11.

1852

Appeal of the Association of Fairfield West, to the Associated Ministers Connected with the General Association of Connecticut. New York: Printed for the Association, 1852.

"New England Theology [I]." *Church Review and Ecclesiastical Register* 5 (October 1852) 349–60.

1853

[Hodge, Charles.] "Doctrinal and Ecclesiastical Conflicts in Connecticut." *Biblical Repertory and Princeton Review* 25 (October 1853) 598–637.

"New England Theology [II]." *Church Review and Ecclesiastical Register* 6 (April 1853) 82–100.

1854

"A Creedless Faith and a Faithless Creed." *Church Review and Ecclesiastical Register* 7 (October 1854) 337–50.

A Protest of the Pastoral Union to the Pastors and Churches of Connecticut. Adopted at a meeting held in Wethersfield, Conn., October 24–25, 1854. [Wethersfield?, 1854?].

Wallace, Benjamin. "Religion and Philosophy." *Presbyterian Quarterly Review* 2 (March 1854) 655–87.

1855

Noyes, George Rappall. "Scripture Doctrine of Sacrifice." *Christian Examiner and Religious Miscellany* 59, 4th s. 24 (September 1855) 234–80.

1856

Thompson, J. W. "Dr. Bushnell on 'Christian Trinity a Practical Truth.'" *Christian Examiner and Religious Miscellany* 60, 4th s. 24 (March 1856) 161–88.

1857

Goodrich, Samuel G. *Recollections of a Lifetime.* Vol. 2. New York and Auburn: Miller, Orton, and Mulligan, 1857.

1858

[Atwater, Lyman H.] "Jonathan Edwards and the Successive Forms of New Divinity." *Biblical Repertory and Princeton Review* 30 (October 1858) 585–620.

1859

Bartol, Cyrus A. "Dr. Bushnell and Dr. Furness: A Question of Words and Names." *Christian Examiner* 66, 5th s. 4 (January 1859) 112–24.

Dana, James D. "Anticipations of Man in Nature: Review of Chapter VII of *Nature and the Supernatural,* by Horace Bushnell." *New Englander* 17 (May 1859) 293–334.

"Dr. Bushnell's Parting Words." *New Englander* 17 (August 1859) 787.

Gage, William Leonard. *Trinitarian Sermons Preached to a Unitarian Congregation.* Boston: J. P. Jewett; Cleveland: H. P. B. Jewett, 1859.

Goodwin, Henry M. "Dr. Bushnell's *Sermons for the New Life.*" *New Englander* 17 (May 1859) 382–99.

Lord, David N. "Dr. Bushnell's Nature and the Supernatural." *Theological and Literary Journal* 11 (January 1859) 529–76.

Nevin, John Williamson. "Notice of *Nature and the Supernatural,* by Horace Bushnell." *Mercersburg Review* (April 1859). Reprinted almost in its entirety in *The Life and Work of John Williamson Nevin,* by Theodore Appel. Pp. 529-50.

Porter, Noah. "Nature and the Supernatural." *New Englander* 17 (February 1859) 224–58.

1861

"Dr. Bushnell's *Character of Jesus.*" *New Englander* 19 (April 1861) 519.

Goodwin, Henry M. "Dr. Bushnell's *Christian Nurture.*" *New Englander* 19 (April 1861) 474–95.

1863

Chase, Irah. *Infant Baptism, Bushnell's Arguments Reviewed.* Philadelphia: American Baptist Publication Society, 1863.

Frothingham, Octavius Brooks. "Renan's Life of Jesus." *Christian Examiner* 75, 5th s. 13 (November 1863) 313–39.

1864

Gage, William Leonard. *Light in Darkness; or, Christ Discovered in His True Character, by a Unitarian.* Boston: Gould and Lincoln, 1864.

1865

Allen, J. H. "Bushnell's *Christ and His Salvation.*" *Christian Examiner* 78, 5th s. 16 (January 1865) 127–28.

"Review of *Christ and His Salvation, in sermons variously related thereto,* by Horace Bushnell." *Atlantic Monthly* 15 (March 1865) 377–78.

1866

Allen, J. H. "Open Questions in Theology." *Christian Examiner* 80, n.s. 1 (January 1866) 77–90.

Andrews, W. W. *Remarks on Dr. Bushnell's Vicarious Sacrifice.*" Hartford: Case, Lockwood, 1866.

"Bushnell on the Vicarious Sacrifice." *Independent* 18 (15 February 1866) 2.

Clarke, James Freeman. "Bushnell on Vicarious Sacrifice." *Christian Examiner* 80, n.s. 1 (May 1866) 360–77.

"God in our History." *Christian Examiner* 81, n.s. 2 (July 1866) 1–16.

James, Henry, Sr. "Review of *The Vicarious Sacrifice.*" *North American Review* 102 (April 1866) 556–71.

Park, Edwards Amasa. "Review of Horace Bushnell's *The Vicarious Sacrifice*." *Bibliotheca Sacra* 23 (April 1866) 345–50.

Porter, Noah. "Review of Dr. Bushnell on *The Vicarious Sacrifice*." *New Englander* 25 (April 1866) 228–82. Reprint. New Haven: n.p., 1866.

"Review of Bushnell's *Vicarious Sacrifice*." *Methodist Quarterly Review* 48 (July 1866) 350–70.

"Review of *The Vicarious Sacrifice*, by Horace Bushnell." *New Englander* 25 (January 1866) 160–62.

T[owne], E. C. "[Review of] *The Vicarious Sacrifice* . . . , by Horace Bushnell." *Christian Examiner* 80, n.s. 1 (March 1866) 276–80.

1867

Gladden, Washington. "Are Dr. Bushnell's Views Heretical?" *Independent* 19 (17 October 1867) 1.

Hodge, Archibald Alexander. *The Atonement*. 1867. Reprint. Grand Rapids: Eerdmans, 1953.

1869

James, William. "Review of Bushnell's *Women's Suffrage* and J. S. Mill's *The Subjection of Women*." *North American Review* 109 (October 1869) 556–65.

1870

Means, John O. "Recent Theories on the Origin of Language." *Bibliotheca Sacra* 27 (January 1870) 162–79.

1871

Crawford, Thomas Jackson. *The Doctrine of Holy Scripture respecting the Atonement*. Edinburgh and London: William Blackwood and Sons, 1871.

1872

Hovey, Alvah. *God with us; or Person and Work of Christ, with an examination of "The Vicarious Sacrifice" of Dr. Bushnell*. Boston: Gould and Lincoln, 1872.

1873

Hoppin, J. M. "Bushnell's *Sermons on Living Subjects*." *New Englander* 31 (January 1873) 95–109.

1874

"Review of *Forgiveness and Law, Grounded in Principles Interpreted by Human Analogies*, by Horace Bushnell." *Methodist Quarterly Review* 56 (July 1874) 583–86.

1875

Dale, Robert William. *The Atonement: The Congregational Union Lecture for 1875*. 18th ed. London: Congregational Union of England and Wales, 1896.

1876

Phelps, Austin. "A Vacation with Dr. Bushnell." *Christian Union* 14 (12 July 1876) 24; 14 (19 July 1876) 47–48.

SECTION 3

Works Written After 1876

Abbott, Lyman. *The Life and Literature of the Ancient Hebrews*. Boston and New York: Houghton, Mifflin, 1901.

_____ . "The Life of Horace Bushnell." *Outlook* (14 October 1899) 413–15.

_____ . *Reminiscences*. Boston and New York: Houghton, Mifflin, 1915.

Adamson, William R. *Bushnell Rediscovered*. Philadelphia and Boston: United Church Press, 1966.

Addison, Daniel Dulany. *Clergy in American Life and Letters*. New York: Macmillan, 1900.

Ahlstrom, Sydney. "Comment on the Essay of Professor Clebsch: History, Bushnell, and Lincoln." *Church History* 30 (June 1961) 223–30.

_____ . "Horace Bushnell." In *A Handbook of Christian Theologians*, edited by Dean G. Peerman and Martin E. Marty. Cleveland and New York: World, Meridian Books, 1967. Pp. 36–39.

_____ . *A Religious History of the American People*. New Haven: Yale University Press, 1972.

_____ . "Theology in America: A Historical Survey." In *The Shaping of American Religion*, edited by James Ward Smith and A. Leland Jamison. Princeton: Princeton University Press, 1961. Vol. 1, pp. 232–321.

_____ , ed. *Theology in America: The Major Protestant Voices from Puritanism to Neo-orthodoxy*. Indianapolis: Bobbs-Merrill, 1967.

Allen, Alexander Viets Griswold. *Freedom in the Church or the Doctrine of Christ*. New York: Macmillan, 1903.

_____ . *The Life of Phillip Brooks*. 2 vols. New York: E. P. Dutton, 1900.

_____ . *Religious Progress*. Boston: Houghton, Mifflin; Cambridge: Riverside Press, 1895.

Allen, Joseph Henry. *Our Liberal Movement in Theology*. Boston: Roberts Brothers, 1882; 3d ed., 1892. Reprint. New York: Arno Press, 1972.

Allen, Walter. "Horace Bushnell." *Atlantic Monthly* 85 (March 1900) 415–25.

Appel, Theodore. *The Life and Work of John Williamson Nevin*. Philadelphia: Reformed Church Publishing House, 1889. Reprint. New York: Arno Press and New York Times, 1969.

Archibald, Warren Seymour. *Horace Bushnell*. Hartford: Edwin Valentine Mitchell, 1930.

Atkins, Gaius Glenn. "New England Theology." *Encyclopedia of Religion*, edited by Vergilius Ferm. New York: Philosophical Library, 1945.

_____ , ed. *Master Sermons of the Nineteenth Century*. Chicago and New York: Willett, Clark, 1940.

_____ , and Fagley, Frederick L. *History of American Congregationalism*. Boston and Chicago: Pilgrim Press, 1942.

Atonement in Modern Religious Thought: A Theological Symposium [Articles from *Christian World* (1899–1900)]. London: James Clarke, 1900.

Atwater, Lyman H. "Horace Bushnell." *Presbyterian Review* 2 (1881) 114–44.

Aubrey, Edwin Ewart. "Religious Bearings to the Modern Scientific Movement." In *Environmental Factors in Christian History: In Honor of Shirley Jackson*

Case, edited by John Thomas McNeill, Mathew Spinka, and Harold R. Willoughby. Chicago: University of Chicago Press, 1939. Pp. 361–79.

Averill, Lloyd. *The New Theology in the Liberal Tradition*. Philadelphia: Westminster, 1967.

Bacon, Benjamin Wisner. *The Apostolic Message: A Historical Inquiry*. New York: Century, 1925.

——————. "The New Theology." *Church Union* 24 (January 1898) 360–63.

——————. *Theodore Thornton Munger, New England Minister*. New Haven: Yale University Press; London: Humphrey Milford/Oxford University Press, 1913.

Bacon, Leonard Woolsey. "Concerning a Recent Chapter of Ecclesiastical History." *New Englander* 38 (September 1879) 701–12.

——————. *A History of American Christianity*. American Church History, edited by Philip Schaff et al., vol. 13. New York: Charles Scribner's Sons, 1907.

Bainton, Roland H. *Yale and the Ministry*. New York: Harper, 1957.

Baird, Robert Dahlin. "Horace Bushnell: A Romantic Approach to the Nature of Theology." *Journal of Bible and Religion* 33 (July 1965) 229–40.

——————. "Religion is Life: An Inquiry into the Dominating Motif in the Theology of Horace Bushnell." Ph.D. dissertation, State University of Iowa, 1964.

Barnes, Howard Andrew. "Horace Bushnell: An American Gentleman." Ph.D. dissertation, University of Iowa, 1970.

——————. "The Idea that Caused a War: Horace Bushnell versus Thomas Jefferson." *Journal of Church and State* 16 (Winter 1974) 73–83.

Bartlett, Irving Henry. "Bushnell, Cousin, and Comprehensive Christianity." *Journal of Religion* 37 (April 1957) 99–104.

——————. "The Romantic Theology of Horace Bushnell." Ph.D. dissertation, Brown University, 1952.

Bartol, Cyrus A. "Dr. Horace Bushnell and the Quandaries of our Theology." *Unitarian Review* 14 (September 1880) 236–48.

——————. "Bushnell the Theologian." In *Principles and Portraits*. Boston: Roberts Brothers, 1880. Pp. 366–85.

Beach, David Nelson. *A Handbook of Homiletics*. Bangor: John H. Bacon, 1912.

——————. *Newer Religious Thinking*. Boston: Little, Brown, 1893.

Bedell, George C.; Sandon, Leo; and Wellborn, Charles T. *Religion in America*. New York: Macmillan, 1975.

Billings, Mildred Kitto. "The Theology of Horace Bushnell Considered in Relation to That of Samuel Taylor Coleridge." Ph.D. dissertation, University of Chicago, 1960.

Billington, Ray A. *The Protestant Crusade, 1800–1860. A Study of the Origins of American Nativism*. New York: Macmillan, 1938. Reprint. Chicago: Quadrangle Books, 1964.

Blau, Joseph Leon, ed. *American Philosophic Addresses, 1799–1900*. New York: Columbia University Press, 1946.

Boardman, George N. *The History of New England Theology*. New York: A. D. F. Randolph, 1899.

Bodo, John R. *The Protestant Clergy and Public Issues, 1812–1848*. Princeton: Princeton University Press, 1954.

Boorman, John Arthur. "A Comparative Study of the Theory of Human Nature as Expressed by Jonathan Edwards, Horace Bushnell, and William Adams Brown." Ph.D. dissertation, Columbia University, 1954.

Bos, A. David. "Horace Bushnell through his Interpreters: A Transitional and Formative Figure." *Andover Newton Quarterly* 18 (November 1977) 122–32.

Brastow, Lewis Orsmund. *Representative Modern Preachers.* New York: Macmillan, 1904.

Brauer, Jerald C. *Protestantism in America: A Narrative History.* Rev. ed. Philadelphia: Westminster Press, 1965.

Brooklyn Eagle, 2 June 1902. [Report of the Centennial Observance of Horace Bushnell's Birth at Plymouth Church, Brooklyn, New York].

Brown, Charles Reynolds, *They Were Giants.* New York: Macmillan, 1934.

Brown, Jerry Wayne. *The Rise of Biblical Criticism in America, 1800–1870: The New England Scholars.* Middletown, CT: Wesleyan University Press, 1969.

Brown, William Adams. *Beliefs That Matter: A Theology for Laymen.* New York: Charles Scribner's Sons, 1928.

—————— . *Christian Theology in Outline.* New York: Charles Scribner's Sons, 1906.

—————— . *The Church in America: A Study of the Present Condition and Future Prospects of American Protestantism.* New York: Macmillan, 1922.

—————— . *God at Work: A Study of the Supernatural.* New York: Charles Scribner's Sons, 1933.

—————— . *How to Think of Christ.* New York: Charles Scribner's Sons, 1945.

—————— . *Imperialistic Religion and the Religion of Democracy: A Study in Social Psychology.* London: Hodder and Stoughton, 1923.

—————— . *The Life of Prayer in a World of Science.* New York: Charles Scribner's Sons, 1927.

Buckham, John Wright. *Progressive Religious Thought in America.* Boston: Houghton, Mifflin, 1919.

Burgraaff, Winfield. *The Rise and Development of Liberal Theology in America.* New York: Board of Publication and Bible Work of the Reformed Church in America, n.d.

Burr, Nelson R. *A Critical Bibliography of Religion in America.* Religion in American Life, edited by James Ward Smith and A. Leland Jamison, vol. 1, pts. 3–5. Princeton Studies in American Civilization, 5. Princeton: Princeton University Press, 1961.

Burton, Ernest DeWitt; Smith, John Merlin; Smith, Gerald Birney. *Biblical Ideas of Atonement: Their History and Significance.* Chicago: University of Chicago Press, 1909.

Burton, Nathaniel J. "Horace Bushnell: An Address Delivered on the Occasion of the Unveiling of a Bushnell Memorial Tablet in Park Church, Hartford, November 24, 1878." In *Yale Lectures,* edited by Richard E. Burton. New York: C. L. Webster and Co., 1888. Pp. 415–29.

—————— . "The North Congregational Church." In *Memorial History of Hartford County,* edited by M. J. Burton. Boston: Edward L. Osgood, 1880. Vol. 1, p. 390.

Bushnell Centenary: Minutes of the General Association of Connecticut at the One Hundred and Ninety-Third Annual Meeting Held in Hartford, June 17–18,

1902. Hartford: Case, Lockwood, and Brainard, 1902. [Seven addresses: see Chesebrough, A. S.; Clark, C. H.; McKinley, C. E.; Munger, T. T.; Mutch, W. J.; Parker, E. P.; Walker, W.].

"Bushnell, Horace." *Dictionary of American Religious Biography,* edited by Henry Warner Bowden. Westport, CT: Greenwood Press, 1977.

"Bushnell, Horace." *New Schaff-Herzog Encyclopedia of Religious Knowledge,* edited by Samuel MacCauley Jackson. New York: Funk & Wagnalls, 1908–14.

"Bushnelliana." *Congregationalist and Christian World* 87 (2 June 1902) 811.

"Bushnell's Value for Today." *Congregationalist and Christian World* 87 (2 June 1902) 806–7.

Butler, J. Donald. *Religious Education: Foundations and Practice of Nurture.* New York and Evanston: Harper and Row, 1962.

Cairns, Earle E. *Christiantity Through the Centuries: A History of the Christian Church.* Grand Rapids: Zondervan, 1954.

Campbell, Dennis M. *Authority and the Renewal of American Theology.* Philadelphia: United Church Press, 1976.

Carpenter, F. B. "Studio Talks with Dr. Horace Bushnell." *Independent* 112 (11 January 1900) 116–20.

Carter, Paul A. *The Decline and Revival of the Social Gospel: Social and Political Liberalism in American Protestant Churches, 1920–1940.* Ithaca, NY: Cornell University Press, 1954. Reprint. Hamden, CT: Shoe String Press, 1971.

_____ . *The Spiritual Crisis of the Gilded Age.* DeKalb: Northern Illinois University Press, 1971.

Case, Adelaide T. "Christian Education." In *The Church Through Half a Century: Essays in Honor of William Adams Brown,* edited by Samuel McCrea Cavert and Henry P. Van Dusen. New York: Charles Scribner's Sons, 1930. Pp. 227–64.

Caskey, Marie. *Chariots of Fire: Religion and the Beecher Family.* New Haven: Yale University Press, 1978.

Cauthen, Kenneth. *The Impact of Religious Liberalism.* New York: Harper and Row, 1966.

Cave, Sydney. *The Doctrine of the Work of Christ.* Nashville: Cokesbury, 1937.

Cecil, Anthony C., Jr. *The Theological Development of Edwards Amasa Park: Last of the "Consistent Calvinists."* American Academy of Religion Dissertation Series, 1. Missoula, MT: American Academy of Religion/Scholars Press, 1974.

Chadwick, John White. "Munger's Bushnell." *Nation* 69 (10 October 1899) 318.

_____ . *Theodore Parker: Preacher and Reformer.* Boston: Houghton, Mifflin; Cambridge; Riverside Press, 1900.

_____ . *William Ellery Channing.* Boston: Houghton, Mifflin, 1903.

Chapman, E. M. "God's Way with a Soul: A Review of Dr. Munger's Horace Bushnell." *Congregationalist and Christian Mirror* 84 (21 September 1899) 396–97.

Cherry, Conrad. *Nature and the Religious Imagination: From Edwards to Bushnell.* Philadelphia: Fortress, 1980.

_____ . "The Structure of Organic Thinking: Horace Bushnell's Approach to Language, Nature, and Nation." *Journal of the American Academy of Religion* 40 (March 1972) 3–20.

Chesebrough, Amos Sheffield. "Reminiscences of the Bushnell Controversy." In *Bushnell Centenary: Minutes of the General Association of Connecticut . . . ,* pp. 47–57.

_____ . "The Theological Opinions of Horace Bushnell as related to his Character and Christian Experience." *Andover Review* 6 (August 1886) 113–30.

Cheyney, Mary Bushnell. *The Life and Letters of Horace Bushnell*. New York: Harper and Brothers, 1880. Reprint. New York: Arno Press, 1969.

Clark, Charles Hopkins. "Bushnell the Citizen." In *Bushnell Centenary: Minutes of the General Association of Connecticut . . .* , pp. 58–69.

Clebsch, William A. *American Religious Thought: A History*. Chicago History of American Religion, edited by Martin E. Marty. Chicago: University of Chicago Press, 1973.

_____ . "Baptism in Blood: Christian Contributions to the Interpretation of the Civil War in American History." Th.D. dissertation, Union Theological Seminary, 1957.

_____ . "Christian Interpretations of the Civil War." *Church History* 30 (June 1961) 212–21. Reprint. Philadelphia: Fortress Press, Facet Books, 1969.

Coe, George Albert. *Education in Religion and Morals*. Chicago: Fleming H. Revell, 1904.

_____ . *Religion of a Mature Mind*. Chicago: Fleming H. Revell, 1902.

_____ . *A Social Theory of Religious Education*. New York: Charles Scribner's Sons, 1927.

_____ . *What is Christian Education?* New York: Charles Scribner's Sons, 1929.

_____ . *What is Religion Doing to our Consciences?* New York: Charles Scribner's Sons, 1943.

Cole, Charles C., Jr. "Horace Bushnell and the Slavery Question." *New England Quarterly* 23 (March 1950) 19–30.

_____ . *The Social Ideas of the Northern Evangelists, 1826–1860*. Columbia Studies in the Social Sciences, 580. New York: Columbia University Press, 1954. Reprint. New York: Octagon Books, 1966.

Congregationalist and Christian World 87 (7 June 1902). See "Bushnelliana"; "Bushnell's Value for Today"; Egleston, H. H.; Gibbon, J. M.; Kelley, W. V.; Munger, T. T.; Parker, E. P.; Thomas, Reuen; Twichell, J. T.; "Personal Indebtedness to Bushnell: Twelve Testimonials."

Crosby, Donald A. *Horace Bushnell's Theory of Language, in the Context of Other Nineteenth-Century Philosophies of Language*. The Hague: Mouton, 1975.

Cross, Barbara M. *Horace Bushnell: Minister to a Changing America*. Chicago: University of Chicago Press, 1958.

Cully, Iris. *The Dynamics of Christian Education*. Philadelphia: Westminster, 1958.

_____ , and Cully, Kendig Brubaker. *Process and Relationship*. Birmingham: Religious Education Press, 1978.

Daniels, Vincent. "Nature and the Supernatural: A Study in the Development of the Thought of Horace Bushnell." Ph.D. dissertation, Yale University, 1939.

DeJong, Peter Y. *The Covenant Idea in New England Theology, 1620–1847*. Grand Rapids: Eerdmans, 1945.

Denny, James. *The Christian Doctrine of Salvation*. 3d ed. Greenwood, SC: Attic Press, 1956.

Dillenberger, John, and Welch, Claude. *Protestant Christianity, Interpreted through its Development*. New York: Charles Scribner's Sons, 1954.

Dinsmore, Charles Allen. *Atonement in Literature and Life*. Boston and New York: Houghton, Mifflin; London: Archibald Constable, 1906.

_____ . "Bushnell, Horace." *Dictionary of American Biography*, edited by Allen Johnson. New York: Charles Scribner's Sons, 1928–58.

Dole, Charles. "Horace Bushnell and His Work for Theology." *New World* 8 (December 1899) 699–714.

Dorn, Jacob Henry. *Washington Gladden; Prophet of the Social Gospel*. N.p.: Ohio State University Press, 1966.

Douglas, Ann. *The Feminization of American Culture*. New York: Alfred A. Knopf, 1977.

Drew. G. S. "An American Divine: Horace Bushnell." *Contemporary Review* 35 (August 1879) 815–31.

Dryer, George Herbert. *History of the Christian Church*. Vol. 5: *The Advance of Christendom, 1800–1901 A.D.* Cincinnati: Jennings & Pye; New York: Eaton & Mains, 1903.

Dunham, Chester Forrester. *The Attitude of the Northern Clergy Toward the South, 1860–1865*. Toledo, OH: Gray, 1942.

Dunning, Albert E. *Congregationalists in America*. New York: J. A. Hill, 1894.

Durba, Arlo D. "The Principles of Theological Language in the Writings of Horace Bushnell and Paul Tillich, and Their Implications for Christian Education Theory." Ph.D. dissertation, Princeton Theological Seminary, 1960.

Durfee, Harold A. "Language and Religion: Horace Bushnell and Rowland G. Hazard." *American Quarterly* 5 (Spring 1953) 57–70.

Dwight, Timothy, Jr. *Memories of Yale Life and Men, 1854–1899*. New York: Dodd, Mead, 1903.

Dyer, John. "Dr. Horace Bushnell." *Penn Monthly* 7 (April 1876) 287–97.

Eakin, Frank, and Eakin, Mildred. "Christian Nurture: A Century After." *Religious Education* 44 (May-June 1949) 136–40.

Egleston, N. H. "Recollections of a Former Parishioner." *Congregationalist and Christian World* 87 (7 June 1902) 820–21.

Fallaw, Wesner. "The Role of the Home in Religious Nurture." In *Religious Education*, edited by Marvin J. Taylor. New York and Nashville: Abingdon Press, 1960.

Feidelson, Charles. *Symbolism and American Literature*. Chicago: University of Chicago Press, 1953.

Fisher, George Park. *Essays on the Supernatural Origin of Christianity, with special reference to the Theories of Renan, Strauss, and the Tübingen School*. New York: Charles Scribner's Sons, 1886.

_____ . *The Grounds of Theistic and Christian Belief*. New York: Charles Scribner's Sons, 1902.

_____ . *A History of Christian Doctrine*. 2d ed. Edinburgh: T. and T. Clark, 1896.

_____ . *History of the Christian Church*. New York: Charles Scribner's Sons, 1928.

_____ . "Horace Bushnell." *International Review* 10 (January 1881) 13–25.

_____ . *The Nature and Method of Revelation*. New York: Charles Scribner's Sons, 1890.

_____ . *An Unpublished Essay of Edwards on the Trinity*. New York: Charles Scribner's Sons, 1903.

Foard, Lawrence Clinton. "The Copernican Revolution in Theology: Studies of the Critical and Romantic Elements in the Theory of Religious Language Proposed by Horace Bushnell." Ph.D. dissertation, Temple University, 1970.

Foster, C. R. "Horace Bushnell on Education." D.Ed. dissertation, Columbia University, 1971.

Foster, Frank Hugh. *A Genetic History of the New England Theology*. Chicago: University of Chicago Press, 1957.

_____ . "Horace Bushnell as a Theologian." *Bibliotheca Sacra* 19 (October 1902) 601–22.

_____ . *The Modern Movement in American Theology: Sketches in the History of American Protestant Thought from the Civil War to the World War*. New York: Fleming H. Revell, 1939.

Franks, Robert Sleightholme. *The Atonement: The Dale Lectures for 1933*. London: Oxford University Press/Humphrey Milford, 1934.

Fredrickson, George M. *The Black Image in the White Mind*. New York: Harper and Row, 1971.

_____ . *The Inner Civil War*. New York: Harper and Row, 1965.

Gabriel, Ralph Henry. *The Course of American Democratic Thought*. New York: Ronald Press, 1940.

_____ . "Evangelical Religion and Popular Romanticism in Early Nineteenth-Century America." *Church History* 19 (March 1950) 37–47.

Gardiner, Edward Clinton. "Horace Bushnell's Concept of Responses: A Fresh Approach to the Doctrine of Ability and Inability." *Religion in Life* 27 (Summer-Autumn 1957–58) 119–31.

_____ . "Horace Bushnell's Doctrine of Depravity." *Theology Today* 12 (April 1955) 10–26.

_____ . "Man as Sinner in Nineteenth Century New England Theology." Ph.D. dissertation, Yale University, 1952.

Garrison, Winifred E. *The March of Faith: The Story of Religion in America since 1865*. New York and London: Harper and Brothers, 1933.

Gaustad, Edwin Scott, ed. *Religious Issues in American History*. Harper Forum Books, edited by Martin E. Marty. New York, Evanston, and London: Harper and Row, 1968.

Gibbon, J. Morgan. "Horace Bushnell's Influence in England." *Congregationalist and Christian World* 87 (7 June 1902) 819–20.

Gladden, Washington. *The Christian Pastor and the Working Church*. New York: Charles Scribner's Sons, 1898.

_____ . "Horace Bushnell and Progressive Orthodoxy." In *Pioneers of Religious Liberty in America*. Boston: American Unitarian Association, 1903. Pp. 227–63.

_____ . *Present-Day Theology*. Boston: Pilgrim Press, 1913.

_____ . *Recollections*. Boston: Houghton, Mifflin; Cambridge: Riverside Press, 1909.

Goodwin, Henry M. *Christ and Humanity*. New York: Harper and Brothers, 1875.

_____ . "Horace Bushnell." *New Englander* 39 (December 1880) 803–27; 40 (January 1881) 1–39.

Gordon, George Angier. *Aspects of the Infinite Mystery*. Boston and New York: Houghton, Mifflin; Cambridge: Riverside Press, 1903.

——————. *The Christ of Today*. Boston and New York: Houghton, Mifflin, 1895.

——————. "The Collapse of the New England Theology." *Harvard Theological Review* 1 (April 1908) 127–68. Reprint. *Humanism in New England Theology*. Boston and New York: Houghton, Mifflin; Cambridge: Riverside Press, 1920.

——————. *The Genius of the Pilgrim*. New York and Boston: Pilgrim Press, 1913.

——————. *My Education and Religion: An Autobiography*. Boston and New York: Houghton, Mifflin, 1925.

——————. *The New Epoch for Faith*. Boston and New York: Houghton, Mifflin; Cambridge: Riverside Press, 1901.

——————. *Religion and Miracle*. London: James Clark, 1909–10.

——————. *Ultimate Conceptions of Faith*. Boston and New York: Houghton, Mifflin; Cambridge: Riverside Press, 1903.

Gray, Joseph M. *Prophets of the Soul*. Reprint. Freeport, NY: Books for Libraries Press, 1971.

Great Thoughts (London) (November 1899) 260–62. [Review of Munger's *Life of Horace Bushnell*].

Grensted, Lawrence William. *A Short History of the Doctrine of the Atonement*. Manchester: At the University Press; London and New York: Longmans, Green, 1920.

——————, ed. *The Atonement in History and in Life: A Volume of Essays*. London: SPCK: New York: Macmillan, 1936 (c. 1929).

Greven, Philip. *The Protestant Temperament*. New York: Alfred A. Knopf, 1977.

Grover, Norman LaMotte. "The Church and Social Action in Finney, Bushnell, and Gladden." Ph.D. dissertation, Yale University, 1957.

Gunn, Giles, ed. *New World Metaphysics: Readings in the Religious Meaning of the American Experience*. New York: Oxford University Press, 1981.

Hammar, George. *Christian Realism in Contemporary American Theology*. Uppsala: A. b. Lundequistska Bokhandeln, 1940.

Handy, Robert T. *A Christian America: Protestant Hopes and Historical Realities*. New York: Oxford University Press, 1971.

——————. *A History of the Churches in the United States and Canada*. Oxford History of the Christian Church. New York: Oxford Unversity Press, 1977.

Harpole, Ralph D. "The Development of the Doctrine of the Atonement in American Thought from Edwards to Horace Bushnell." Ph.D. dissertation, Yale University, 1924.

Harris, George. *A Century's Change in Religion*. Boston and New York: Houghton, Mifflin, 1914.

Harris, Samuel. *God: Creator and Lord of All*. 2 vols. New York: Charles Scribner's Sons, 1896.

——————. *The Self-Revelation of God*. New York: Charles Scribner's Sons, 1886.

The Hartford Times, 27 October 1937. ["Bushnell Memorial Edition."]

Heiniger, Harold Richel. "The Theological Technique of a Mediating Theologian— Horace Bushnell." Ph.D. dissertation, University of Chicago, 1935.

Henderlite, Rachel. "The Theological Basis of Horace Bushnell's Christian Nurture." Ph.D. dissertation, Yale University, 1947.

Herbst, Jürgen. *The German Historical School in American Scholarship: A Study in the Transfer of Culture.* Ithaca, NY: Cornell University Press, 1965.

Hodge, Charles. *Systematic Theology.* Vol. 2. Reprint. Grand Rapids: Eerdmans, 1975.

Holifield, E. Brooks. *The Gentlemen Theologians: American Theology in Southern Culture, 1795-1860.* Durham, NC: Duke University Press, 1978.

Holland, DeWitte Talmadge, ed. *Preaching in American History: Selected Issues in the American Pulpit, 1630-1967.* New York and Nashville: Abingdon, 1969.

_____ . ed. *Sermons in American History: Selected Issues in the American Pulpit, 1630-1967.* Nashville and New York: Abingdon, 1971.

Homrighausen, E. O. "Christian Theology and Christian Education." *Religious Education* 44 (November–December 1949) 353–63.

Hopkins, Charles Howard. *The Rise of the Social Gospel in American Protestantism, 1865-1915.* Yale Studies in Religious Education, 14. New Haven: Yale University Press; London: Humphrey Milford/Oxford University Press, 1940.

Horton, Walter Marshall. "Eugene W. Lyman; Liberal Christian Thinker." In *Liberal Theology, An Appraisal: Essays in Honor of Eugene William Lyman,* edited by David E. Roberts and Henry Pitney Van Dusen. New York: Charles Scribner's Sons, 1942. Pp. 3–44.

_____ . *Realistic Theology.* New York and London: Harper and Brothers, 1934.

Hough, Lynn Harold. *The Quest for Wonder, and Other Philosophical and Theological Studies.* New York: Abingdon, 1915.

Howell, John Edmond. "A Study of the Theological Method of Horace Bushnell and its Application to his Cardinal Doctrines." Ph.D. dissertation, Duke University, 1963.

Hoyt, Arthur S. *The Pulpit and American Life.* New York: Macmillan, 1921.

Hudson, Winthrop S. *The Great Tradition of the American Churches.* New York: Harper and Brothers, 1953.

_____ , ed. *Nationality and Religion in America: Concepts of American Identity and Mission.* Harper Forum Books, edited by Martin E. Marty. New York and Evanston: Harper and Row, 1970.

_____ . *Religion in America: An Historical Account of the Development of American Religious Life.* New York: Charles Scribner's Sons, 1965; 3d ed., 1981.

Hutchison, William R. *The Modernist Impulse in American Protestantism.* Cambridge: Harvard University Press, 1976.

_____ . *Transcendentalist Ministers: Church Reform in the New Engand Renaissance.* New Haven: Yale University Press, 1959. Reprint. Boston: Beacon Press, 1965.

Johnson, William Alexander. "Horace Bushnell Revisited: A Study of the Development of His Theology." *Drew Gateway* 35 (Autumn 1964) 10–38.

_____ . *Nature and the Supernatural in the Theology of Horace Bushnell.* Studia Theologica Lundensia, 25. Lund: Gleerup, 1963.

_____ . "Nature and the Supernatural in the Theology of Horace Bushnell." *Encounter* 26 (Winter 1965) 65–74.

Jones, Howard Mumford. *The Age of Energy: Varieties of American Experience, 1865-1915.* New York: Viking Press, 1970.

_____ . "The Influence of European Ideas in Nineteenth-Century America." *American Literature* 7 (March–January 1935–36) 241–73.

Keller, Charles R. *The Second Great Awakening in Connecticut.* New Haven: Yale University Press, 1952.

Kelley. W. V. "A Preacher's Preacher." *Congregationalist and Christian World* 87 (7 June 1920) 821.

Kirschenmann, Frederick. "Horace Bushnell: Cells or Crustacea?" In *Reinterpretations in American Church History*, edited by Jerald C. Brauer. Chicago: University of Chicago Press, 1968. Pp. 67–89.

_____ . "Horace Bushnell: Orthodox or Sabellian?" *Church History* 33 (March 1964) 49–59.

Kleiser, Grenville, comp. *The World's Great Sermons.* Vol. 4. New York: Funk and Wagnalls, 1908.

Knott, Garland. "Bushnell Revisited." *Religious Education* 64 (July 1969) 291–96.

Knudten, Richard. *The Systematic Thought of Washington Gladden.* New York: Humanities Press, 1968.

Krahn, John H. "Nurture versus Revival: Horace Bushnell on Religious Education." *Religious Education* 70 (July–August 1975) 375–82.

Latourette, Kenneth Scott. *A History of Christianity.* Vol. 2: *Reformation to the Present.* Rev. ed. New York: Harper and Row, 1975.

_____ . *A History of the Expansion of Christianity.* Vol. 4: *The Great Century in Europe and the United States of America, A.D. 1800–A.D. 1914.* New York: Harper and Row, 1941.

Learned, John C. "Dr. Bushnell." *Unity* 5 (July–August 1880) 158–59, 177–79.

Lewis, R. W. B. *The American Adam: Innocence, Tragedy, and Tradition in the Nineteenth Century.* Chicago: University of Chicago Press, 1955.

Lidgett, John Scott. *The Spiritual Principle of Atonement.* 4th ed. London and Robert Culley, [1897].

Lo, Eddie Bong. "Horace Bushnell's Epistemology in Relation to his Major Christian Doctrines: A Historical, Philosophical, and Theological Consideration." Ph.D. dissertation, Claremont College, 1977.

Lyman, Eugene William. "Christian Thought and a Spiritualist Philosophy." In *Contemporary American Theologians*, edited by Vergilius Ferm. New York: Round Table Press, 1932–33. Vol. 2, pp. 105–31.

_____ . *The Experience of God in Modern Life.* New York: Charles Scribner's Sons, 1918.

Lynn, Robert W. *Protestant Strategies in Education.* New York: Association Press, 1964.

MacFayden, Dugald. "Bushnell, Horace." *Encyclopedia of Religion and Ethics*, edited by James Hastings. New York: Charles Scribner's Sons. 1908.

McGiffert, Arthur Cushman, Jr. "Protestant Liberalism." In *Liberal Theology, An Appraisal: Essays in Honor of Eugene William Lyman*, edited by David E. Roberts and Henry Pitney Van Dusen. New York: Charles Scribner's Sons, 1942. Pp. 106–20.

_____ . *The Rise of Modern Religious Ideas.* New York: Macmillan, 1915.

Macintosh, Robert. *Historic Theories of Atonement, with Comments.* London, New York, and Toronto: Hodder and Stoughton, 1920.

McKinley, Charles E. "Bushnell and Christian Nurture: The Doctrine." In *Bushnell Centenary: Minutes of the General Association of Connecticut* . . . , pp. 100–10.

Maclear, James Fulton. "'The True American Union' of Church and State: The Reconstruction of the Theocratic Tradition." *Church History* 28 (March 1959) 41–62.

McLoughlin, William G. *The Meaning of Henry Ward Beecher: An Essay on the Shifting Values of Mid-Victorian America, 1840–1870*. New York: Knopf, 1970.

_____ . *Modern Revivalism; Charles Grandison Finney to Billy Graham*. New York: Ronald Press, 1959.

_____ , ed. *American Evangelicals, 1800–1900: An Anthology*. New York and Evanston: Harper and Row, Harper Torchbooks, 1968.

Marsden, George M. *The Evangelical Mind and the New School Presbyterian Experience: A Case Study of Thought and Theology in Nineteenth Century America*. New Haven and London: Yale University Press, 1970.

Marty, Martin. *Righteous Empire: The Protestant Experience in America*. Two Centuries of American Life: A Bicentennial Series, edited by Harold M. Hyman and Leonard W. Levy. New York: Dial Press, 1970.

May, Henry C. *Protestant Churches and Industrial America*. New York: Harper and Brothers, Harper Torchbooks, 1949.

Mead, Charles Marsh. *Supernatural Revelation: An Essay Concerning the Basis of the Christian Faith*. New York: Anson D. F. Randolph, 1889.

Mead, Edwin D. "Editor's Table: Horace Bushnell, The Citizen." *New England Magazine*, n.s. 21 (December 1899) 505–16.

Mead, Sidney E. *The Lively Experiment: The Shaping of Christianity in America*. New York, Evanston, and London: Harper and Row, 1963.

Meland, Bernard. "A Critical Analysis of the Appeal to Christ in Present-Day Religious Interpretations." Ph.D. dissertation, University of Chicago, 1929.

Meyer, Daniel Harvey. *The Instructed Conscience*. Philadelphia: University of Pennsylvania Press, 1972.

Miller, Perry. *Errand into the Wilderness*. New York: Harper and Row, Harper Torchbooks, 1964.

Miller, Randolph Crump. *The American Spirit in Theology*. Philadelphia: Pilgrim Press, 1974.

_____ . *Biblical Theology and Christian Education*. New York: Charles Scribner's Sons, 1956.

_____ . *Christian Nurture and the Church*. New York: Charles Scribner's Sons, 1961.

_____ . *The Clue to Christian Education*. New York: Charles Scribner's Sons, 1950.

_____ . *Education for Christian Living*. Englewood Cliffs, NJ: Prentice-Hall, 1956.

_____ . "God's Gift to the Imagination." *Perkins Journal* 32 (Spring 1979) 9–16.

_____ . *Guide for Church School Leaders*. Louisville: Cloisters Press, 1947.

_____ . "Horace Bushnell: Prophet to America's Children." *Perkins Journal* 32 (Spring 1979) 1–8.

_____ . *The Language Gap and God*. Philadelphia and Boston: Pilgrim Press, 1970.

—————. "A State Renewed in Righteousness." *Perkins Journal* 32 (Spring 1979) 17–25.

—————. *This We Can Believe.* New York: Hawthorn Books, 1976.

—————. *Your Child's Religion.* Garden City: Doubleday, 1962.

Minnick, Wayne C. "Horace Bushnell: Precursor of General Semantics." *ETC* 5 (1947–48) 246–51.

Mitchell, Donald G. *American Lands and Letters.* New York: Charles Scribner's Sons, 1899.

Moore, Edward Caldwell. *An Outline of the History of Christian Thought since Kant.* New York: Charles Scribner's Sons, 1912.

Moorhead, James H. *American Apocalypse: Yankee Protestants and the Civil War, 1860–1869.* New Haven: Yale University Press, 1978.

Mozley, John Kenneth. *The Doctrine of the Atonement.* New York: Charles Scribner's Sons, 1916.

Munger, Theodore Thornton. "The Aphorisms of Horace Bushnell." *Congregationalist and Christian World* 87 (7 June 1902). Reprinted in Horace Bushnell, *The Spirit in Man,* pp. 405–44.

—————. "Horace Bushnell." In *A Library of the World's Best Literature, ancient and modern,* edited by Charles Dudley Warren. New York: International Society, 1897. Vol. 7, pp. 2909–26.

—————. "Horace Bushnell." In *Christendom Anno Domini MDCCCCI: A Presentation of Christian Conditions, etc.,* edited by William D. Grant. New York: Chauncy Holt, 1902. Vol. 2, pp. 120–27.

—————. ["Horace Bushnell"]. In *Prophets of the Christian Faith: A Series of Essays.* New York: Macmillan, 1896. Pp. 169–92.

—————. "Horace Bushnell: The Centenary of a Great Alumnus." *Yale Alumni Weekly,* 9 April 1902.

—————. "Horace Bushnell: A Correction." *Yale Alumni Weekly,* 23 April 1902.

—————. *Horace Bushnell: Preacher and Theologian.* Boston: Houghton, Mifflin, 1899.

—————. "Memorial Sermon." Reprint from *The Pacific* (San Francisco) in *The Courant* (Hartford), 10 April 1876.

—————. "The Secret of Horace Bushnell." *Outlook* 71 (30 August 1902) 1063–68; also in *Bushnell Centenary: Minutes of the General Association of Connecticut . . . ,* pp. 35–46.

Munro, Harry Blyde. *Protestant Nurture.* Englewood Cliffs, NJ: Prentice-Hall, 1956.

Mutch, William J. "Bushnell and Christian Nurture: The Mode." In *Bushnell Centenary: Minutes of the General Association of Connecticut . . . ,* pp. 111–21.

Myers, A. J. William. *Horace Bushnell and Religious Education.* Boston: Manthorne and Burdock, 1937.

Nichols, James Hastings. *Romanticism in American Theology: Nevin and Schaff at Mercersburg.* Chicago: University of Chicago Press, 1961.

Niebuhr, Helmut Richard. *The Kingdom of God in America.* New York: Harper and Brothers, 1937; Harper Torchbooks, 1959.

Niswonger, Donald. "Nature and the Supernatural as Reflected in the Theological Works and Sermons of Horace Bushnell." S.T.M. thesis, Union Theological Seminary, 1961.

Nott, C. C. "Dr. Bushnell." *Nation* 31 (9 August 1880) 136–37.

Orr, James. *The Christian View of God and the World Centering in the Incarnation, being the first series of Kerr Lectures [1890–91].* Grand Rapids: Eerdmans, 1948.

Paine, Levi Leonard. *A Critical History of the Evolution of Trinitarianism and its Outcome in the New Christology.* Boston and New York: Houghton, Mifflin, 1900.

Park, Edwards Amasa. "Recollections of Henry Boynton Smith." In *Henry Boynton Smith: His Life and Work,* edited by Elizabeth Lee Smith. New York: Armstrong and Son, 1881. Pp. 127–35, 143–44.

Parker, Edwin Pond. "Dr. Bushnell's Marks in Hartford." *Congregationalist and Christian World* 87 (7 June 1902) 817–18.

──────── . *The Hartford Central Association and the Bushnell Controversy.* Hartford: Published for the Association by Case, Lockwood, and Brainard Co., 1896.

──────── . "Horace Bushnell: Christian Prophet." In *Bushnell Centenary: Minutes of the General Association of Connecticut . . .* , pp. 86–99.

Paul, Robert S. *Atonement and the Sacraments.* New York and Nashville: Abingdon, 1960.

Paul, Sherman. "Horace Bushnell Reconsidered." *ETC* 6 (1948–49) 255–59.

Pearson, Samuel C. "All Things New: Images of Man in Early Nineteenth-Century America." *Encounter* 35 (Winter 1974) 1–13.

"Personal Indebtedness to Bushnell: A Symposium." *Congregationalist and Christian World* 87 (7 June 1902) 815–16.

Persons, Stow. "Religion and Modernity, 1865–1914." In *The Shaping of American Religion,* edited by James Ward Smith and A. Leland Smith. Princeton: Princeton University Press, 1961. Vol. 1, pp. 369–401.

Phelps, Austin. *My Portfolio.* New York: Charles Scribner's Sons, 1882.

──────── . *The Theory of Preaching: Lectures on Homiletics.* New York: Charles Scribner's Sons, 1891.

Porter, Noah. "Horace Bushnell: A Memorial Sermon Preached in the Chapel of Yale College, Sunday, March 16th, 1876." *New Englander* 36 (January 1877) 152–69.

──────── . "Philosophy in Great Britain and America, A Supplementary Sketch." In *A History of Philosophy,* by Friedrich Überweg. Vol. 2. *History of Modern Philosophy, with Additions.* Translated by George S. Morris. Theological and Philosophical Library, edited by Henry Boynton Smith and Philip Schaff. New York: Scribner, Armstrong, 1877.

Qualben, Lars Pederson. *A History of the Christian Church.* New York: Thomas Nelson and Sons, 1936.

The Religious History of New England: King's Chapel Lectures. Cambridge: Harvard University Press; London: Humphrey Milford/Oxford University Press, 1917.

Riegler, Gordon Arthur. *The Socialization of the New England Clergy, 1800–1860.* Perspectives in American History 37. Philadelphia: Porcupine Press, 1979.

Robbins, Kirk W. "The Writings of Horace Bushnell as an Approach to a Theology for Christian Nurture." Ph.D. dissertation, Drew University, 1938.

Rynin, David, ed. *Alexander Bryan Johnson's "A Treatise on Language [1836]."* Berkeley; University of California Press, 1947.

Salmond, Stewart D. F. "Review of *Horace Bushnell: Preacher and Theologian*, by T. T. Munger." *London Quarterly Review* 94, n.s. 4 (July–October 1900) 310–26.

——————. "The Theology of Horace Bushnell." *London Quarterly Review* 95, n.s. 5 (January–April 1901) 133–58.

Schaff, Philip. *Christ and Christianity*. New York: Charles Scribner's Sons, 1885.

Schlesinger, Arthur M., and White, Morton, eds. *Paths of American Thought*. Boston: Houghton, Mifflin, 1963.

Schneider, Herbert W. *A History of American Philosophy*. 2d ed. New York and London: Columbia University Press, 1963.

Schneider, Robert Allen. "Form, Symbol, and Spirit: Religious Knowledge in the Thought of Horace Bushnell." M.A. thesis, Pennsylvania State University, 1974.

Selbie, W. B. *Congregationalism*. London: Methuen, 1927.

Sheldon, Henry Clay. *The History of Christian Doctrine*. 2 vols. Cincinnati: Jennings and Graham; New York: Eaton and Mains, 1885.

——————. *The History of the Christian Church*. Vol. 5 New York and Boston: Thomas Y. Crowell, 1894.

——————. *The System of Christian Doctrine*. Cincinnati: Jennings and Graham; New York: Eaton and Mains, 1903.

Smith, Chad Powers. *Yankees and God*. New York: Hermitage House, 1954.

Smith, David. *Atonement in the Light of History and the Modern Spirit*. London and New York: Hodder and Stoughton, n.d.

Smith, David L. *Symbolism and Growth: The Religious Thought of Horace Bushnell*. American Academy of Religion Dissertation Series, 36. Chico, CA: American Academy of Religion/Scholars Press, 1981.

Smith, Gerald Birney. *Social Idealism and the Changing Theology*. New York: Macmillan, 1913.

Smith, Henry Boynton. *Introduction to Christian Theology: Apologetics*. 2 vols. in one. Edited by William S. Karr. New York: A. C. Armstrong and Son, 1897.

——————. *The System of Christian Theology*, edited by William S. Karr. New York: A. C. Armstrong and Son, 1884.

Smith, Hilrie Shelton. *Changing Conceptions of Original Sin: A Study in American Theology Since 1750*. New York: Charles Scribner's Sons, 1958.

——————. *Faith and Nurture*. New York: Charles Scribner's Sons, 1941.

——————, ed. *Horace Bushnell: Twelve Selections*. A Library of Protestant Thought. New York: Oxford University Press, 1965.

——————; Handy, Robert T.; and Loetscher, Lefferts, eds. *American Christianity: An Historical Interpretation with Representative Documents*. 2 vols. New York: Charles Scribner's Sons, 1960–63.

Smith, Timothy L. *Revivalism and Social Reform: American Protestantism on the Eve of the Civil War*. New York: Harper and Row, Harper Torchbooks, 1965.

Smyth, Newman. *The Orthodox Theology of Today*. New York: Charles Scribner's Sons, 1881.

Spindell, Verne A. "The Influence of Samuel Taylor Coleridge on Nineteenth-Century American Religious Thought." Ph.D. dissertation, University of Chicago, 1941.

Starkey, Marion L. *The Congregational Way: The Role of the Pilgrims and their Heirs in Shaping America*. Garden City: Doubleday, 1966.

Stearns, Lewis French. *The Evidence of Christian Experience*. New York: Charles Scribner's Sons, 1911.

——————. *Henry Boynton Smith*. American Religious Leaders. Boston and New York: Houghton, Mifflin; Cambridge: Riverside Press, 1893.

Stephens, Bruce M. *God's Last Metaphor: The Doctrine of the Trinity in New England Theology*. American Academy of Religion Studies in Religion, 24. Chico, CA: American Academy of Religion/Scholars Press, 1981.

——————. "Horace Bushnell and the New England Theology." *Dialog* 14 (Fall 1975) 268–73.

Stevens, George Barker. *The Christian Doctrine of Salvation*. International Theological Library, edited by Charles Augustus Briggs and Stewart D. F. Salmond. New York: Charles Scribner's Sons, 1911.

——————. "Horace Bushnell and Albrecht Ritschl: A Comparison." *American Journal of Theology* 6 (January 1902) 32–56.

——————. "The Theology of Horace Bushnell." *Methodist Review* 84 (September 1902) 692–707.

Steward, David Stanley. "Bushnell's Nurture Process: An Exposition." *Religious Education* 64 (July 1969) 296–302.

——————. "Horace Bushnell and Contemporary Christian Education: A Study of Revelation and Nurture." Ph.D. dissertation, Yale University, 1966.

Stewart. George. *A History of Religious Education in Connecticut to the Middle of the Nineteenth Century*. New Haven: Yale University Press; London: Humphrey Milford/Oxford University Press, 1924.

Stockbridge, J. C. "Bushnell, Horace." In *Cyclopaedia of Biblical, Theological, and Ecclesiastical Literature*, edited by John M'Clintock and James Strong. New York: Harper, 1891.

Stoever, William K. B. "Henry Boynton Smith and the German Theology of History." *Union Seminary Quarterly Review* 24 (Fall 1968) 69–89.

Stokes, Anson Phelps. *Memorials of Eminent Yale Men*. Vol. 1. New Haven: Yale University Press, 1914.

Stowe, Lyman Beecher. *Saints, Sinners and Beechers*. Indianapolis: Bobbs-Merrill, 1934.

Strong, Augustus Hopkins. *Systematic Theology: A Compendium designed for the Use of Theological Students, 1886*. 3d ed., 3 vols. in one. Philadelphia: Judson Press, 1907.

Strong, Josiah. *Our Country: Its Possible Future and Its Present Crisis*. New York: Baker and Taylor Co., for the American Home Missionary Society, 1891.

Sweet, William Warren. "The Frontier in American Christianity." In *Environmental Factors in American Christianity*, edited by John Thomas McNeill, Mathew Spinka, and Harold Willoughby. Chicago: University of Chicago Press, 1939. Pp. 380–98.

——————. *Makers of Christianity from John Cotton to Lyman Abbott*. New York: Henry Holt, 1937.

——————. *Religion in the Development of American Culture, 1765–1840*. New York: Charles Scribner's Sons, 1952.

——————. *The Story of Religions in America*. New York: Harper and Brothers, 1930.

Swift, David Everett. "Conservative versus Progressive Orthodoxy in Latter 19th Century Congregationalism." *Church History* 16 (March 1947) 22–31.

Thomas, Reuen. "My Week with Bushnell." *Congregationalist and Christian World* 87 (7 June 1902) 813–14.

Thompson, Ernest T. *Changing Emphases in American Preaching*. Philadelphia: Westminster, 1943.

Towne, Elmer T. "Horace Bushnell." In *A History of Religious Educators*, edited by Elmer T. Towne. Grand Rapids: Baker, 1975. Pp. 278–87.

Trumbull, Henry Clay. *My Four Religious Teachers*. Philadelphia: Sunday School Times, 1903.

——————. "Reminiscences of Dr. Bushnell." *Sunday School Times*, 5 and 12 August and 2 September 1899. Reprint. Philadelphia: n.p., 1899.

——————. *Teaching and Teachers*. Philadelphia: John D. Wattles, 1884.

Trumbull, James Hammond, ed. *The Memorial History of Hartford County, Connecticut, 1663–1884*. Vol. 1. Boston: Edward L. Osgood, 1886.

Tucker, William Jewett. *My Generation: An Autobiographical Interpretation*. Boston and New York: Houghton, Mifflin; Cambridge: Riverside Press, 1919.

Tuveson, Ernest Lee. *Redeemer Nation: The Idea of America's Millennial Role*. Chicago and London: University of Chicago Press, 1968.

Twichell, Joseph H. "A Word from Another Hartford Disciple." *Congregationalist* (Boston), 7 June 1902.

——————. "Dr. Bushnell in the Woods." *Outlook* 65 (2 June 1900) 261–65.

——————. "Personal Reminiscences." In *Bushnell Centenary: Minutes of the General Association of Connecticut . . .* , pp. 70–85.

"Two American Divines: Dr. Bushnell and Dr. Mühlenberg." *Appleton's Journal*, n.s. 9 (September 1880) 277–88.

Van Dusen, Henry Pitney. "The Liberal Movement in Theology." In *The Church Through Half a Century: Essays in Honor of William Adams Brown*, edited by Samuel McCrea Cavert and Henry Pitney Van Dusen. New York: Charles Scribner's Sons, 1930. Pp. 65–90.

Vieth, Paul H. *The Church and Christian Education*. St. Louis: Bethany Press, 1947.

——————. *Objectives in Religious Education*. New York: Harper and Brothers, 1930.

Walker, Williston. "Dr. Bushnell as a Religious Leader." In *Bushnell Centenary: Minutes of the General Association of Connecticut . . .* , pp. 15–34.

——————. "Bushnell, Horace." *Encyclopaedia Britannica*. 11th ed. Cambridge: University Press, 1910–11.

——————. "Changes in Theology among American Congregationalists." *American Journal of Theology* 10 (April 1906) 204–18.

——————. *Great Men of the Christian Church*. Chicago: University of Chicago Press, 1908.

——————. *A History of the Congregational Churches in the United States*. American Church History Series, 3. New York: Charles Scribner's Sons, 1894.

——————. *Ten New England Leaders*. New York, Boston, and Chicago: Silver, Burdett, 1901.

Weeks, Lewis. "Horace Bushnell on Black America." *Religious Education* 68 (1973) 28–41.

Weigle, Luther A. "Bushnell, Horace." *Encyclopedia of Religion*, edited by Vergilius Ferm. New York: Philosophical Library, 1945.

_____ . "The Christian Ideal of Family Life as Expounded in Horace Bushnell's *Christian Nurture*." *Religious Education* 19 (1924) 47–57.

_____ . *The Glory Days: From the Life of Luther Allan Weigle*. Compiled by Richard R. Weigle. New York: Friendship Press, 1976.

_____ . *The Pageant of American Idealism*. New Haven: Yale University Press, 1928.

_____ . "The Religious Education of a Protestant." In *Contemporary American Theologians*, edited by Vergilius Ferm. New York: Round Table Press, 1933. Vol. 2, pp. 311–40.

Weisenburger, Francis P. *The Ordeal of Faith: The Crisis of Church-Going America, 1865–1900*. New York: Philosophical Library, 1959.

Weiss, John. *The Life and Correspondence of Theodore Parker*. Vol. 2. New York: D. Appleton, 1864.

Welch, Claude. *Protestant Thought in the Nineteenth Century. Vol. 1: 1799–1870*. New Haven and London: Yale University Press, 1972.

Williams, Daniel Day. *The Andover Liberals*. New York: Kings Crown Press, 1941. Reprint. New York: Octagon Books, 1970.

_____ . "Tradition and Experience in American Theology." *The Shaping of American Religion*, edited by James Ward Smith and A. Leland Johnson. Princeton: Princeton University Press, 1961. Vol. 1, pp. 443–75.

Yale Alumni Weekly, 20 October 1901. Printed as pamphlet, *Yale Alumni Weekly, . . . The Bicentennial . . . Issue of Commemoration*. New Haven: n.p., 1902. [Addresses: Fisher, George Park, "Theologians of Yale"; Gilman, Daniel C., "The Relations of Yale to Letters and Science"].

INDEX